CLIMATE SOLUTIONS

Current & Emerging Hopeful Options

Maia Ballis

Dedication

This book is dedicated with heartfelt gratitude to our precious planet, which sustains a diverse array of life forms, including humanity. I envision a livable, greener future for ourselves and generations yet to come.

Special thanks to the Fresno Unitarian Universalist Church environmental community for their enthusiastic encouragement of this project. It is my hope that this work informs and inspires positive choices that contribute to actions that mitigate climate change while fostering a more equitable global bioeconomy.

About the Author

Maia Ballis has a passion for the environment that aligned with that of her husband, George Ballis, a renowned documentary photographer and filmmaker celebrated for his compelling farm labor imagery.

In 1974, they co-created a small organic co-op farm in Fresno before moving to the Sierra foothills in 1983, where they designed and built the first solar-electric building in Fresno and demonstrated energy-conservation equipment at SunMt Environmental Research Center.

There, they researched low-water-use plants and continued to grow and market organically sustainable crops. Maia is a fine artist, photographer and graphic designer with a background in interior design. She has cultivated her knowledge of herbology, exploring innovative ways to incorporate their seasonal herbs, edible flowers and native plants into products for market.

Maia shared health-conscious culinary creations with visitors during monthly food exploration meals and taught classes on making her natural, non-toxic body care products. For over five decades, she has written numerous articles to increase public awareness about the food system, herbology and holistic health, alternative energy, and energy conservation.

Foreword

I know we can save our planet and make it livable for all sentient beings, and after you read this book, you will know it too. Together, we can build the momentum needed to make choices that support the most Earth-friendly options to mitigate climate change.

Even if you don't believe in climate change, after reading this information, you may also come to understand that a circular bioeconomy makes economic as well as environmental sense. It can create local hubs of self-sufficiency with a broader impact, making us more water, food, and fuel self-sufficient in an era of volatile geopolitics.

I have been environmentally conscious for over half a century. I've made many behavioral changes and researched, tried, and written about climate-friendly options beyond buying an electric or hybrid car, which many people can't afford.

Recently, I was saddened to learn that the grim environmental realities still don't activate enough people into working on climate change, but that there is now a term called "climate suicide" for environmental studies students who become so fearful, hopeless and depressed about their future that they kill themselves.

My Unitarian Universalist Church Fresno congregation chose to reduce their family's carbon footprint by 5,000 pounds in 2008. They did and we also have a LEED-certified green sanctuary building and an energy-conscious campus.

I offered a Zoom meeting to my environmental committee to share some of the most exciting and hopeful emerging options I knew about. Participants in that meeting were so enthusiastically appreciative and filled with hope that I realized this book was needed.

Herein are many options. May we choose well.

TABLE OF CONTENTS

Chapter One
GREENING EARTH

What Is

The Bioeconomy?

The Bioeconomy is an economic model that uses renewable biological resources from land and sea, such as microorganisms, crops, and forests, to produce energy, food, natural fibers, and other biological materials. It aims to drive sustainable development in a circular cycle of regeneration by converting these resource "waste streams" into value-added products. At the same time, innovations in this process have high potential to mitigate climate change while creating a more sustainable and resilient bioeconomy.

Addressing climate change requires concerted efforts to target these key contributors by reducing emissions, enhancing carbon sinks, and transitioning to more sustainable practices across all sectors. We have strategies to mitigate climate change that have often focused on transitioning to renewable energy sources, improving energy efficiency, promoting sustainable land use and agriculture, and optimizing waste management practices. Understanding these contributors helps prioritize actions that can have the most significant impact on reducing greenhouse gas emissions and combating climate change.

This book was written to share existing and exciting emerging technologies that offer great hope and the many options that individuals have. Climate change is driven by human activities. Humans can make different choices.

GHG SOURCES

Fossil Fuel Combustion

Most people are aware that burning coal, oil, and natural gas for electricity, heat, and transportation is the largest source of atmospheric global greenhouse gas (GHG) emissions, releasing carbon dioxide (CO_2), methane (CH_4), and nitrous oxide (N_2O), significantly contributing to global warming. We have other options.

California Energy Leadership

California, under Governor Gavin Newsom, is actively addressing the severe impacts of climate change, including fires, droughts, and erosion from heavy rains. The state's strategy focuses on resilience and includes robust clean air and water regulations, alongside substantial investments in renewable energy, utility-scale battery storage, and green job creation.

This commitment to green energy has not only promoted environmental sustainability but also spurred economic growth, making California an attractive hub for innovative companies in the renewable sector. The state has made significant infrastructure advancements, with 201,000 public electric vehicle chargers now available, surpassing the 120,000 gas stations. Since 2019, California's renewable energy capacity has expanded significantly. Currently, 67% of the state's energy comes from clean sources, and it achieves carbon-free energy generation for 9 out of 10 days.

Climate Action Progress

On July 4, 2025, former US Vice President Al Gore gave a TED talk on why rising climate action is unstoppable. He pointed out that the world has installed twice as much solar energy as all fossil fuels combined since 2015. Renewable energy sources like solar power offer advantages over fossil fuels, including job creation, stable fuel costs, and environmental benefits. Renewable energy investments are increasing rapidly, while fossil fuel markets are projected to decline. Annual electric vehicle (EV) sales have increased 34-fold since the Paris Agreement, with China accounting for 52% of those sales. More proportional global investment in renewables is needed in developing countries like Africa, where solar and wind could provide 100% energy access with minimal land use.

He said the fossil fuel industry is the main obstacle to the transition to renewable energy. Removing direct fossil fuel subsidies could save $4.4 trillion, which could finance the transition to renewables. But the powerful fossil fuel industry opposes any regulations aimed at addressing their GHG emissions. Instead, they promote carbon credits and get global tax dollars spent on costly carbon capture and storage, which are diversions to justify continued fossil fuel use. But voter demands for renewables can oppose their lobbying power. Gore reminds us that political will is a renewable resource, and that individuals can vote and buy EVs and solar panels. But we can also do other things.

Agriculture

Agricultural practices, including livestock production and the use of synthetic fertilizers, currently contribute significantly to greenhouse gas emissions. Livestock produce methane through digestion (enteric fermentation), and fertilizers release nitrous oxide, both are potent GHGs, but we have a solution.

There is an agricultural soil amendment that improves long-term soil health, structure, water retention, and enhanced nutrient uptake, and creates more resilient crops, reducing the need for chemical inputs. That can decrease reliance on synthetic fertilizers and pesticides. These and other green options offer the most important unexplored solutions to climate change mitigation if used widely.

Waste Management

Landfills and waste decomposition release potent GHG methane if biological materials are not properly managed, exacerbating the greenhouse effect. Advanced continuous fermentation composting can turn the biological "waste" stream from landfills and agriculture into a more profitable revenue stream, well enhancing soil health.

Deforestation

The clearing of forests for agriculture, logging, and urban expansion reduces the number of trees that can absorb CO_2 from the atmosphere. Promoting sustainable practices, such as eco-friendly agriculture and forestry, and conserving existing forests through protected areas can help.

We have advanced biological systems for restoring degraded land to plant more trees. Construction lumber demand contributes to deforestation, but we can grow mixed-use plantations of the fastest-growing trees on Earth. Individuals can support policies that enforce regulations and help by reducing their own paper and palm oil consumption, choosing certified wood products, and supporting conservation groups.

Industrial Processes: There are high-impact solutions for current industrial production. Manufacturing and metal processing, which emit various GHGs, including CO_2, methane, and fluorinated gases, account for a substantial percentage of global emissions. We have current and emerging options for these problems.

Transportation: The transportation sector, including road, air, rail, and maritime transport, primarily relies on fossil fuels, generating significant emissions. The combustion of diesel and gasoline fuels from vehicles results in substantial CO_2 emissions and other pollutants that contribute to climate change. We currently have renewable biofuels that reduce emissions, public rail and EVs from trucks, buses, and cars to e-bikes, scooters & skateboards, and Robo EV taxis. New generations of batteries that are more efficient and use no rare earth are emerging.

Energy Production

Aerosols and Black Carbon, the particulate matter from burning fossil fuels and biomass, can influence climate patterns and contribute to warming effects. Renewable energy sources are on the rise. Energy production will include biomass-derived fuel for biochar production and biological carbon storage through composting. Renewable energy sources such as solar, hydro, wind, and new nuclear can replace fossil fuels.

Construction & Industry: Buildings consume energy predominantly from fossil fuels. Our built environment accounts for nearly 40% of total daily global emissions. Energy-conscious building codes and technological shifts are slowly reducing them. Leadership in Energy and Environmental Design (LEED)- certified green buildings are growing in popularity. Over 195,000 projects were LEED certified worldwide as of 2024. Supply chain optimization and better equipment maintenance can also contribute to reducing emissions.

Lifestyles: Needed policy changes will take time, but we can progress by holding corporations accountable and pressing for climate justice. But we can also look in the mirror to see what more we can do as individuals. Use the current options described in this book and be informed about emerging technologies. All the choices we make about how we eat, travel, work, manage our homes, choose hobbies, and engage in entertainment have environmental implications.

There is much that individuals can do to address climate change. What will your next step be?

Chapter Two
Magical Pear Tree Farm

The classic Magical Pear Tree story is about a priest who asked a man with a pear tree for a piece of fruit, but the man refused. But a kind man bought a pear for the priest, who ate the pear, saved the seeds, and returned them to the buyer. Those seeds produced a prolific pear tree that bore a great amount of fruit.

We thought the farm was a "Tree of Possibilities" that needed to be fertilized with generosity, hope, and action to be fruitful. For business, we condensed the name of our 7-acre co-op to Pear Tree Farm.

I have been working on small-farm survival for 50 years and on climate-related solutions since 1973 through nonprofit work with my now-deceased husband, George "Elfie" Ballis. Later, we created SunMt Environmental Research Center. We educated legislators and got a building permit to allow our research center to demonstrate the first solar-electric power system in Fresno, California.

Deadly Farming

When I was born, DDT was promoted by the government and industry for use as an agricultural and household pesticide. Early concerns about its use evolved into strong opposition after the publication of Rachel Carson's book Silent Spring, which cautioned about potential impacts on the environment and the food system.

Widespread use had been promoted without evaluation of potential negative impacts on human health. Carson told us DDT and other pesticides caused cancer in humans and were a threat to birds. By 1972, it was banned for agricultural use, but it is still used to combat mosquitoes.

When I lived in downtown Fresno, the demolition of houses for the Community Hospital construction brought cockroaches to our neighborhood. After finding roaches all over the ceiling, I bought DDT-laden pesticide and sprayed it from the center of the room, so it fell back on me. The human body can only detox so much, and I was unaware of the toxicity, but I was tired all the time after that and had to drink coffee all day to stay awake.

In 1962, 19 million gallons of the powerful herbicide Agent Orange were sprayed across Vietnam. It stripped plant cover from the enemy and deprived them of food. Exposure continues to damage our troops and over 400,000 Vietnamese and their environment 50 years later.

Post-war, manufacturers reframed those chemicals for agricultural use as a "War on Weeds," perpetuating the myth that herbicides and pesticides could kill insects and weeds without harming humans or the environment. Science eventually revealed that these poisons had very damaging effects on humans, and DDT could affect multiple generations.

It takes seven years for a liver to regenerate. I used liver-protective milk thistle in my coffee substitute recipe with roasted barley, dandelion, and chicory root to help me slowly detoxify and regenerate my liver.

In the 1970s, we couldn't believe that anyone could monopolize the seed market, but Monsanto did. Their genetically modified (GM) seeds required their custom biocides found in Roundup, which they said would only affect weeds and not harm food plants or humans.

Their marketing spread use from farms to gardens, dramatically expanding Roundup use. The Institute for Responsible Technology reported that the water-soluble biocide glyphosate in Roundup can bind essential minerals, weakening plants and harming humans. In 2022, Roundup was linked to an increased risk of B-cell and T-cell non-Hodgkin's lymphoma, liver damage, and neurological disorders. Bayer bought Monsanto, and thousands of people are demanding compensation from the $11 billion lymphoma compensation fund.

For years, my diet has been organic food and filtered water that removes biocides, which dramatically reduces my chemical load. CCOF-certified organic foods accounted for about 6% of 2024 retail food sales, up 5% from the previous year, outpacing conventional food sales, driven by consumer demand for healthier, environmentally friendly products. Organic growing reduces the use of prohibited fossil-fuel-based fertilizers and synthetic pesticides, resulting in a significantly lower carbon footprint.

The xenoestrogens that are in all the weed killers can enter our bodies through food, plastic water bottles, personal care products, household products, and the environment. Tiny amounts accumulate in fat cells over time, overload the human system, and cause health problems. In men, xenoestrogens are proven to cause excess estrogen and low levels of testosterone, a primary cause of prostate cancer and neurodegenerative Parkinson's disease.

Wild & Organic Roots

At Pear Tree Farm, we explored everything we could grow, focusing on resilient plants that require less water and planning for droughts and climate change. We grew certified organic herbs for market, and I developed unusual products to carve out a market niche for us. If you have only tasted supermarket tomatoes and tree fruit, you will be amazed at the actual flavor of food picked ripe from your own plants or from certified growers at farmers' markets.

At certified farmers' markets, you are sure to get food from the actual grower. Most commercial crops are picked unripe for storage and transport time. Tree fruit may look good if it is conventional grown, but it usually has no flavor.

John Ballis hauling produce for market, working bees & farmhouse arbor

Busy Bees Farm

Our son John managed the farm, and we would roll out in the cool of the morning to work in the fields for a few hours, doing whatever John needed to have done that morning. The farm purchased a beehive from a beekeeper to pollinate crops at the Pear Tree.

John needed to split the hive because it grew too large, and then there were two. He married his wife, Lynette, and two years later, they bought 30 hives. They have been caring for bees at their Busy Bees Honey Farm ever since. Their raw honey is one of those ancient superfoods with multiple health benefits that are lost during pasteurization. Honey will last indefinitely, making it non-perishable.

Honey Benefits

Besides being a natural sweetener, raw honey used topically is known to heal wounds as an astringent, a broad-spectrum antibacterial and anti-fungal, and soothing to a sore throat. One tablespoon of raw honey contains about 64 calories with 17 grams of sugar, containing a mix of simple and complex sugars. If your system can handle the sugars, people have been using one teaspoon of raw local honey before bed to help boost immunity to local pollens.

It has antioxidant properties that boost health with anti-inflammatory polyphenols, support digestion, and may have a protective effect on the respiratory, cardiovascular, and nervous systems. Honey is produced when the worker or forager bees gather nectar from various flower sources and take it back to the hive. Once there, the forager transfers it to an inside bee through their proboscis.

During this process, the inside bee produces an enzyme in her mouth that helps dry out the nectar from 23% to 17% moisture level. The nectar is then transferred to cells in the hive, where it finishes drying. The bees seal it with wax made from their abdomens. Then it is ready to be extracted by the beekeeper.

To produce a single pound of honey, the honeybee makes 70,000 trips for nectar.

Currently, John and Lynette are losing one-third or more of their hives to Varroa mite predation and other factors contributing to colony collapse, yet they still use only natural methods to control losses. They share information at local beekeepers' club meetings and at public events.

Adobe Solar Greenhouse & Office

Inspired by Earthships, ancient adobe buildings, and edible landscaping design, we modified the two-car garage into office space, with double French doors opening onto an attached greenhouse, using local adobe bricks for the foundation and south-facing walls. That gave us passive solar winter heat.

Our little energy-efficient wood stove provided any additional winter heat and provided constantly available hot water. The greenhouse panels were removed in summer to form a cooling arbor covered with edible or usable deciduous vines that dropped foliage in winter, allowing solar heat from the greenhouse to enter.

George developed a circular strategy promoted through our nonprofit, where small family farmers could be supported directly by farmers' markets and buyers' co-ops, building larger circles of consumer-farmer connections. We later formed farmers' cooperatives to reach larger markets and, in 1973, helped organize Fresno City into four food-buying clubs with coworker Marc Lasher and his college friend, Susan.

Marc, George, and I worked full-time to organize the buying clubs into a storefront called Our Store. It ran on all volunteer labor from 400 members, allowing for reduced prices on bulk food. Although the food co-ops and buying clubs died in the 2000s, natural food and grocery stores have adopted the use of bulk items in bins to this day, reducing packaging waste and lowering food costs.

Mulching

In the late 1960s, we practiced organic gardening and used Ruth Stout's heavy mulching system from: How to Have a Green Thumb Without an Aching Back. Mulching reduced water use by up to half, blocked weeds, and built soil all at the same time. We continued to mulch and used no-till farming at the Pear Tree Farm.

No-till farming minimizes soil disturbance by planting crops directly into the soil without tilling. By using free leaves from the City of Fresno or buying straw left over from grain harvesting, we heavily mulched our soil afterward.

Marc & Ray move leaf mulch

No-till farming promotes the development of beneficial soil organisms, helps retain soil moisture, improves carbon storage, and reduces greenhouse gas emissions, making it a sustainable approach to agriculture. This practice ultimately leads to healthier ecosystems and can increase crop resilience to varying weather conditions.

CCOF Organic Certification

Organic produce is cultivated without the use of synthetic fertilizers, pesticides, or genetically modified organisms (GMOs), emphasizing sustainable farming practices that promote biodiversity and soil health.

Like a human body's immune system, vigorous, healthy plants are also more resistant to pests and rely on natural IPM pest control. After the required inspection and soil testing for us to become California Certified Organic Farmers, George became the founding treasurer of the CCOF Board of Directors in our region.

COMPOSTING

Composting is the decomposition of organic materials through microbial activity, transforming carbon-rich materials into nutrient-rich compost. John had rabbits he fed from kitchen scraps, composted their manure with straw, and had worm beds he used to help feed our compost pile to rebuild our soil.

The guys used a funnel to urinate into five-gallon tins in the bathroom. The urine was diluted with ten parts water and used to activate compost, or diluted more and used as a nitrogen soil amendment. The strong ammonia smell develops after a day, so daily dumping reduces odor problems.

At the Pear Tree, we expanded composting on our farm. We won an environmental award for recycling all the leaves from the streets of the City of Fresno. The windrows started 17feet high on the front acre, and by spring, they were down to about a foot deep.

The leaf mulch and natural soil amendments helped build rich garden soil rapidly. After a while, we could just bury a day's food scraps in open areas. By the next day, you could dig and see the worms and insects working on breaking down the material.

Landscape gardeners who brought us grass clippings quickly learned that the grass would compost. We passed by where two of them had a cyclone fence, making compost for their own plants. You know you're doing a good thing when they use your idea, so we considered that a success.

Composting is more important now than ever. California passed SB 1383, requiring that in 2022, every residential and commercial business have access to a separate collection of food and yard waste for composting to sequester carbon. Also, SB 54 sets 2032 as a deadline for making all single-use packaging recyclable, working toward removing landfills.

AGROECOLOGY

Chilean-born professor Miguel Altieri from UC Davis was excited to see that we had high-nitrogen leguminous trees planted on the garden perimeters. He explained that it was an ancient traditional Chilean solution for producing nitrogenous matter from the leaves. They would rake the leaf-rich soil from under the trees into areas used for other crops in their systems to rotate crops and naturally build soil nutrition.

Small Farm Support

Marc located all the small farmers selling bulk produce and olive oil from their farms in or near Fresno City, and I created Getting It Straight, a direct marketing map we sold door to door.

Farmers Markets

Marc connected farmers who wanted to sell their produce and developed weekly certified farmers markets in Fresno and Clovis. Certified markets sell only foods produced by the growers, unlike outdoor markets, where vendors simply buy boxes of produce from a local produce house to retail. He organized two farmers' markets that continue to provide fresh local food directly to Fresno and Clovis consumers, supporting rural economies and building community.

Organic Growers Co-op, Marc also created the San Joaquin Valley Farmers Co-op to help small farmers market their organic crops. The co-op worked when operating with the standard fluctuating market pricing. But he asked the markets to agree to pay the same fair price all season. They happily paid a low price in early season (when prices are usually high) but broke the agreement when they could get cheaper prices elsewhere later in the season. We learned that it's hard for producers to change standard supply-and-demand market practices.

The Richest Land

Where does your food come from? The store.

Where does your water come from? The tap.

We take so much for granted that both children and adults often give these answers to questions about the necessities of life. Even farm advisors didn't know how all the crops were being processed.

So, in 1971, George made a short documentary, *The Richest Land*, to quickly educate people about the major issues in agriculture. Now, there is a local public television series called My Job Depends on Ag that features how growers and processors produce a wide variety of crops here.

A friend who was a member of the National Farmers Union (NFU) informed us that farmers earned just three to four cents from each ninety-nine-cent can of tomatoes, highlighting the urgent need for them to receive a fairer share of the profits. Growers found themselves at the bottom of an increasingly consolidated corporate infrastructure and supply chain.

Anticompetitive corporate practices were prevalent across various sectors, including seeds, meatpacking, crop protection, rail transportation, fertilizers, food retailing and distribution, plus the manufacturing and repair of farm equipment.

Microplastic Reduction

Manufacturers seduced us into a throwaway society that was more convenient, but there is no "away" for non-biodegradable products. It is harder to retrain yourself to reduce, reuse, and recycle now. All plastic detritus degrades into microplastics, the foreign substance that scientists have found in the bloodstreams of fish, and at this writing, the average human brain is said to contain a teaspoon of plastic.

Estimates of microplastic levels in humans vary widely, but recent research suggests that adults inhale up to 68,000 microplastic particles per day, which accumulate in organs such as the blood, lungs, liver, and brain. Microplastics can also transfer from plastic food containers, and absorption is increased by heat.

A huge Pacific Garbage Patch island composed of plastic debris floats just below the surface, only visible when you are over it. The mass has been growing for decades and is now estimated to be twice the size of Texas.

Plastic Recycling Reality

Only 9% of all the plastic ever produced has been recycled, and 12% has been incinerated. The rest lies in landfills or has been dumped into the oceans. Biodegradable bags are showing up in my grocery stores and can be used several times before they rip. We encouraged the use of recyclable paper bags and reusable containers for bulk foods at Our Store Food Co-op to reduce plastic use.

California's SB 270 has a single-use carryout bag ban. Stores may sell reusable plastic bags made with recycled content, biodegradable bags, or recycled paper bags. I have been carrying cotton shopping bags for decades, but it took work to remind myself to take them into stores. I was shocked into forming the habit when I learned that even cotton shopping bags have a footprint that requires 17 years of daily use to offset. I'm working on it.

Integated Pest Management

We used Integrated Pest Management (IPM), as promoted by co-founders Bill and Helga Olkowski, which they brought to farms and gardens as an effective, environmentally sensitive pest management approach that prioritizes long-term prevention by combining biological, cultural, and physical techniques.

By applying natural repellents and hand-picking, squashing, or pruning off insects and pests, they are less likely to multiply beyond control. Beneficial insects can more easily keep a natural balance and avoid the need for toxic chemicals. Solutions sometimes included releasing more beneficial insect predators, such as praying mantises or ladybugs, to control the pests. We used biodegradable soap and water, and grew our own Cayenne pepper for topical treatments. These techniques and found that they worked adequately for us in most situations.

Frances Moore Lappé

Diet for a Small Planet by Frankie Lappé, published in 1971, was a seminal influence on our view of the global food system and made us aware of eating lower on the food chain to conserve resources. High-protein animal-based proteins provide all nine essential amino acids the human body needs, including lean meats, but poultry and fish/seafood are lower on the food chain.

She encouraged many converts with her feed grain analysis. Data on the enormity of the resources flowing into livestock production.

Pounds of Feed Grain required to produce one pound of meat:

Beef = 16 lbs.

Pork = 6 lbs.

Turkey = 4 lbs.

Chicken & Eggs = 3lbs.

We stopped eating meat and adopted a vegetarian protein diet of tofu, beans, dairy, eggs, quinoa, oats, nuts, and seeds. We returned to poultry and fish 25 years later when our diet was negatively affecting our health. She saw that people who reluctantly had given up their gas-guzzling cars would never think of questioning the resource costs of their grain-fed-meat diet. Earth could never provide the majority of its people with the grain-fed meat-centered diet Americans take for granted.

People asked her about recipes rather than recognizing that her goal was to explore the roots of global hunger, poverty, and environmental crises, so she wrote a book with co-author Joe Collins called Food First: Beyond the Myth of Scarcity and founded a non-profit by the same name.

Her goal has been to explain that world hunger is rooted in unequal land control and economic pressures, and that we need food democracy to empower citizens and build the inclusive power essential to solving global problems like hunger and climate change. She also co-founded the Small Planet Institute and Small Planet Fund.

Cattle Methane Reduction

Solutions to reducing methane emissions from cattle focus on feed additives such as red seaweed, improved genetics, better manure management, and changes to high-quality forage diets. Research is exploring masks, vaccines, and advanced breeding for sustainable livestock production.

Research shows that red seaweed reduces methane production by inhibiting the microbes in the cow's digestive system that produce methane. Studies have demonstrated that it can cut methane emissions by up to 98% in feedlots and by 37.7% in grazing beef cattle. Studies noted no negative impact on milk production or animal health. This solution is creating a global aquaculture expansion.

Meat & Dairy Alternatives Current meat and dairy alternatives are rapidly gaining popularity as consumers seek sustainable and health-conscious options. Among the most well-known alternatives is tofu, an ancient form of meatless protein soy bean curd discovered in China and favored especially by Buddhist monks. The bland soy-based product can absorb flavors and be prepared in various ways, making it a staple in vegetarian and vegan diets.

There are a number of plant-based meats made from pea protein, lentils, or mushrooms that mimic the texture and taste of traditional meat, appealing to both vegetarians and flexitarians. Seitan, made from wheat gluten, offers another chewy, protein-rich substitute for meat.

Non-dairy beverages include almond, soy, coconut, and oat "milks" which have become popular alternatives to cow's milk, providing lactose-free options with varying flavors and nutritional profiles.

There are also dairy-free innovations like cashew cheese, coconut cheeses and yogurt, and pea protein-based ice creams that deliver both the taste and texture consumers are looking for. This growing market reflects an increasing awareness of environmental impacts, health benefits, and ethical and environmental considerations surrounding animal agriculture, prompting a shift toward diverse and innovative plant-based options.

Chapter Three
SunMt GREEN LIFE

When the City of Fresno expanded to include the Pear Tree Farm, they didn't want our organic farm in the city. So we started looking for a special place to pioneer our evolutionary projects on rural land. We found a 40-acre parcel in Fresno County's Sierra foothills, in the Chaparral zone, with a spectacular 500-foot seasonal waterfall at the upper end.

The land had never been farmed, so we became certified organic growers immediately. We saw the environmental challenges of our time as exciting opportunities for creative innovations to build healthy rural communities. We wanted to demonstrate a possible greener future and regenerative green lifestyle.

We expected to do solar research and demonstration, so our research center was named Sun Mountain, shortened to SunMt. We needed to build a house and barn. So we created a passive-solar-assisted design and educated legislators to get the building department to allow our research center to demonstrate the first solar-electric building in Fresno County, CA, in 1983-4.

That ignited the solar electric industry after the local paper ran an article titled, “Bye Bye PG&E,” which wasn't exactly true. We still used PG&E power to pump our household and irrigation water from a 350 ft-deep well, but our monthly power bill was $12 in 1984.

We also obtained building code approval for the first experimental Clivus Multrum-type composting toilet system, but it has not become popular. Our two toilet options were side-by-side in small closets. The dual low-flush toilet has become more popular.

Now there is a wide variety of energy-conscious toilet options. We continued our plant research and demonstrated organic growing and marketing alternatives with co-worker Marc Lasher and various interns. We marketed certified organic culinary herbs in tea mixtures and sold them alongside our produce.

GREEN BUILDING - SUN HOUSE

We had been researching energy-conservation design for 10 years before we had land to put it to use. I drafted some preliminary plans with input from George's engineering brain, and we took them to an early passive-solar design expert.

He confirmed the viability of our concept and suggested vents on the south wall floor to pull the hot air from the winter sun into the second floor. We incorporated that idea in two ways. We broke the 80-foot-long horizontal "bowling alley" structure into three sections and used:

- Super-insulated floor hatches in the office and the tub room.
- An insulated plenum box with air duct vents in the kitchen kick space.
- A living room French door that opened to the second-story east deck and a two-story greenhouse.

George picked a building site in view of the spectacular winter waterfalls cascading from the 500-foot cliffs, which would be behind and to the east of the structure. The living and dining area had spectacular views of the seasonal waterfalls, but the house would be safe from extreme weather events.

A water-powered electrical system in the falls area ruined the view, so we returned it and opted for a system designed by pioneering solar electrical engineer Don Loweburg, who later became Chair of our nonprofit's Board of Directors.

CONSTRUCTION FEATURES

We used post and beam framing. The two-story shed roof structure had a low end of 10 feet and a high end of 17 feet on the second floor, with clerestory Pella windows that we opened with a long mechanical wand to vent out heat in the summer. We used fire- and insect-resistant redwood or cedar. We recycled 4" x 13" oak timbers from the deconstructed Sun-Maid raisin factory for beefy library vertical supports for shelving and for kitchen countertops.

Greenhouse: Our attached greenhouse also assisted in warming the house in winter. We had dual-pane plexiglass panels that slid into the grooves of the post-and-beam greenhouse construction. We removed them in the summer to prevent added heat and used the framing to create an arbor for grapevines in one section.

Insulating Window & Door Treatments: We had tall, narrow, dual-glazed windows and French doors with large glass panes, for which I designed removable insulating panels of upholstery fabrics.

I sewed magnets around the perimeter that easily attached to a metal French door leading into the greenhouse. That allowed me to moderate the seasonal heat and light. I also used tension rods in the insulated fabric window treatment system, which worked so well that I still use the Reflectix aluminum-faced bubble wrap insulating material to modulate weather extremes in my senior apartment today.

Double-Glazed Skylights: Brought sunlight directly into the center of the house.

Tile Floors: We used tile throughout for durability. Surrounded by gardens that we were in and out of all the time, so tiles were the best solution for dirty boots and heavy traffic from tour groups.

Reflective Roof: We used a white corrugated metal roof with matching corrugated plastic skylights. I later coated the roof with an Arctic white elastomeric protective layer. The white was highly reflective to reduce summer heat. We used samples of roof colors and white as a touch test to demonstrate superiority during house tours. The elastomeric coating also reduced the chance of lightning strikes, which were common in our area and once took out a computer.

Rain Catchment: The roof had rain gutters that channeled water into large concrete cisterns in the greenhouse. That created a cool mass adjacent to the south side of the house that also served as a simple graywater system.

Water: Our water was pumped from a 350-foot-deep water table. We pumped water to a 5,000-gallon tank at the high end of the property and used gravity-fed irrigation to the orchards, gardens, and the house below.

Low-Flush & Composting Toilets: We also pioneered the first legal composting toilet with a low-flush toilet option in the next room, so both could be used simultaneously.

Because they are a biological system that requires more attention than a flush toilet, most people are not willing to put in the effort to maintain a composting toilet, but we did. The two small toilet rooms opened onto the hallway and were next to the laundry room sink or the tub room sink to optimize space for handwashing.

Gray Water: featured two above-ground concrete storage cisterns in the greenhouses that stored rainwater filtered through a modified aluminum cooking pot filled with gravel. That rainwater helped irrigate our gardens south of the house. Now, building codes require far more complicated systems.

Low-Flow Faucet & Shower Head. These fixtures are highly recommended for water conservation. A stained-glass artist friend created a window using a manzanita flower I designed for our composting toilet bathroom window, making it a native plant that offers natural light while obscuring the view from outside.

SOLAR ELECTRIC PIONEERS

We had been planning to use the emerging solar electric technology for over ten years and envisioned a home that could provide its own food, & energy. Gasoline, electricity, and natural gas were expected to become scarce and unaffordable rapidly. The construction of the Diablo nuclear power plant was announced, giving us more incentive to demonstrate the viability of solar electric power.

Don & helper installing rooftop solar panels and second-stage solar equipment.

Pioneering our solar electric power system through the very strict, reluctant Fresno County Building Department was not easy, but our efforts paid off. The carpenters could not believe it when they plugged in their circular saws.

Our system was installed by Don Loweburg of Offline Solar in 1984 and paid for itself in less than ten years, functioned well for over 25 years and the solar panels lasted for 30. Our solar system has given us greater energy security. When PG&E's power was out, our lights, radio, and TV stayed on while the rest of the hillside was dark.

Solar expert Don Loweberg created our dual AC & DC solar electric systems and recommended our 24 Volt ceiling fans, which help move the air down in hot weather and up in cold weather to bring down heat from the ceiling. The invisible but accessible 12V & 24 Volt wiring was run through hollowed-out 2x4s & 4x4s along exposed framing posts on the interior.

Equipment:

DC Sun Frost refrigerator and eventually added an energy-efficient standard refrigerator.

DC Evaporative Cooler: worked well in dry but not humid heat.

Solar Hot Water: We also used a "bread box" passive solar water-heating system that used natural convection to push the hot water up into the house plumbing on the second floor. It was fashioned after a solar box heater project I worked on for the local Indian Rancheria.

The simple design is a plywood box heavily insulated inside and propped at a 45° angle to capture maximum solar gain through a plexiglass lid over two recycled hot water heater tanks painted heat-absorbing black. The interior of the box is also painted black to reduce solar heat gain, and the exterior is painted heat-reflecting white.

Wood Stove Hot Water: Our Canadian Pioneer wood stove had a built-in hot-water reservoir with a spigot at the bottom. Wood-burning stoves do pollute the air, so now people are being discouraged from using them.

Thermos Hot Water: After we learned that in Japan, they heat water once and retain it in a thermos, we did the same.

Countries like Sweden and Germany are heating a large volume of water once and storing it in highly insulated caverns or underground thermos tanks to use on demand later.

Solar Oven & Dryer: We had a solar box oven that I loved in the summer heat. On a deck outside the kitchen, I could slow cook food from bread to baked potatoes, mixed root vegetables to meatloaf in covered black enamel pots. It was the Solar equipment I missed most after leaving SunMt.

The Solar Dryer was similar, but a shallow box with an acrylic lid, wide enough for two cookie sheets, that could be removed from a hatch in the back. I used it to dehydrate fruit and vegetables or to make solar-dried cookies and crackers.

Tankless Water Heaters: We used a Paloma tankless system plumbed so that it allowed inflow from the passive breadbox solar hot water system or from a propane gas-powered hot water on-demand system.

Irrigation Water Conservation: Drip irrigation or Mini sprinkler heads on irrigation lines watered the plants.

Swimming Aquarium: Our 12' x 40' irrigation pond sat just below the water storage tank and doubled as a swimming aquarium/ fish pond. We populated the pond with water hyacinth and edible lotus plants.

Snorkel, a wood-fired hot tub, sat adjacent to the pool and was fired up in wet weather; it worked even in snow. In hot 100°+ weather, George would jump into the water fully clothed, and his clothing became an evaporative cooler while he worked in the garden.

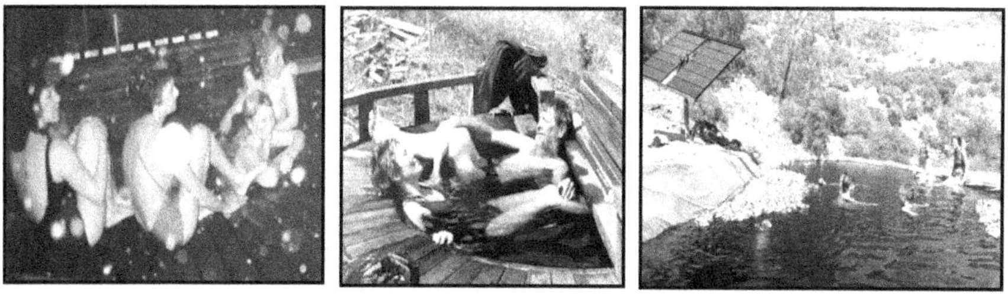

Hot tubbing in the snow, George and Maia with snorkel, woodstove, and irrigation pond.

SUN GARDENS

Fresno County is desert-like with an average high of 9" of rain, and it seldom rains between May & November. SunGardens has many drought-tolerant, pest-resistant, multi-purpose perennials. We were still CCOF-certified organic growers, so we began mulching and planting immediately.

At SunMt, we used Permaculture design concepts. George was looking for drought-tolerant, tough mother plants in expectation of climate change. We grew a variety of drought-tolerant cacti and conducted extensive plant trials of drought-tolerant cultivated and native plants. We published articles and created files on our research, which are archived at the California State University, Fresno, library special collections section.

Our soil fertility program was based on the abundant use of purchased dairy and horse manures, our own composting-toilet humanure, and composted straw and green waste, plus periodic applications of refined sugar and nutritional yeast to feed soil microbes. After soil testing, we balanced soil needs with rock minerals to provide fertility and plant resistance to disease and insect attack, and used standard organic farming techniques. Heavy mulching suppressed weeds while providing soil biomass.

When the system became temporarily unbalanced due to infestations or weather stress, we continued using IPM non-toxic soaps, oils, and a few predatory insects. On occasion, we needed the biological pesticide Bacillus thuringiensis (Bt). A handful of soil may hold 100 billion microorganisms. When they consume the dead bodies of plants, they release valuable mineral nutrients for new cycles of plant life. By collaborating with nature's diversity, we can deliver the safest, highest-quality produce in the marketplace without splicing genes.

GARY NABHAN: Native Seed Search

Saving heirloom seeds is crucial for future food security, biodiversity, and cultural preservation, and for helping food systems adapt to climate change. Ethnobotanist Gary Nabhan of Native Seed/SEARCH, based in hot, arid Tucson, Arizona, helped save & regenerate heirloom seeds adapted to the Sonoran desert.

The Papago People have dwelt in the Sonoran Desert for millennia, using native plants and animals. The health of the Papago was suffering from rising diabetes due to shifting from traditional foods to processed flour and junk foods. Gary Nabhan searched the desert for highly nutritious traditional crops that were falling out of use.

He realized that preserving the seeds could create pride in their traditional Tohono O'odham and Papago heritage, and that their traditional foods would help their health; so he reintroduced more nourishing, high-fiber beans and native plant foods back into their culture.

His dietary work is considered a success in cultural revitalization and a model for addressing modern health crises, such as diabetes, through a "genetically appropriate diet." Gary was also encouraging the indigenous farmers who continued to plant in the old floodplains, capturing the moisture from the rains for irrigation. Adequate water was an issue for them. He helped save their techniques and became an award-winning author of The Desert Smells Like Rain.

Nabhan gave us seeds of wonderful desert crops for our arid-land research: Tepary Beans, Papago White Corn, Mesquite beans, several varieties of Cactus, Desert Melons, Desert Squash, and Devil's Claw.

We grew them all at SunMt. My favorite cactus was the Opuntia, aka. Prickly Pear, or Beavertail, cactus, with bright *red* blossoms and deep purple-red fruit (tunas). The juicy flesh of the flat pad lowers blood sugar and is now officially used to treat diabetes, high cholesterol, obesity, and hangovers. They are yummy cooked in the traditional manner with onion and peppers or chopped fresh for salsa.

I easily removed the spines using a microfiber scrubber and checking under crosslight. I also canned slices with marjoram so they tasted more like green beans. Cholla bud cactus is another favorite. The buds are high in calcium and I created a mineral-rich soup recipe with mushrooms, tofu and Cholla buds.

Nabhan explained that commercial cotton strains need to be periodically reintroduced with DNA from wild varieties to reinvigorate the plants, and that seed banks and plant tissue banks are very important.

See their website to learn about adopting a plant. www.nativeseeds.org

Mesquite: Honey mesquite can live hundreds of years. The hardwood is famous as a preferred source of BBQ fuel, but the pods were a major food source for indigenous people, and the flowers are a prolific pollen source for bees. That drought-tolerant tree was included when we started planting the orchards.

I can now buy organic powdered mesquite beans commercially, but I used to solar-cook and reduce mesquite beans to make a delicious maple-like beverage. It takes 40 gallons of reduced maple sap to make 1 gallon of maple syrup, so solar reducing mesquite bean pods in a solar oven is far more efficient.

Mulberry: We grew a couple of varieties of Mulberry trees. The thornless perennial berry is very sweet. A tarp under the tree captured fallen fruit. I would gather the good berries and shake out the tarp so that overripe berries would compost to feed the tree. The berry colors are purple-black, red or white.

All the blackberries make a purple dye. So never plant them where smashed berries can be tracked on hard surfaces like concrete. Morus Alba is the species favored by silkworms. Silk moth pupae are edible insects, consumed in some cultures.

Jujube: Wanting to grow Jujubes, we made an 800-mile trip to an abandoned field station in Paradise, California, where 17 Jujube trees were surviving with no irrigation. But our attempts to propagate from seed failed. We realized that the mystery tree along the south fence line at Pear Tree Farm was a medicinal-sized Jujube!

The small, very sweet apple-like fruit is high in vitamin C, an antioxidant, and minerals. It is used in Traditional Chinese Medicine (TCM). Jujube is often included in herbal formulas to moderate the effects of other, more potent herbs and to harmonize the body's systems.

It is a detoxifying agent and also used for indigestion, anxiety and insomnia because of sedative effects on the nervous system. A friend had mature, large-fruited Jujubes with suckers in her yard, and she invited us to take some. Propagating by sucker was the best way to go, and thanks to her gift, we had three trees of various forms.

Native & Naturalized Plants George joined the California Native Plant Society and the Rare Fruit Exchange, and we found the local Intermountain native plant nursery, which were all sources for our unusual plants to push the envelope of what we could grow.

COMPOSTING

Our large-capacity CTS brand composting toilet used a single, large chamber to break down human waste into a dry humus. It worked by maintaining an aerobic environment for microbes to decompose reducing its volume by up to 90%. We started out doing the standard compost piles and turning them, as we had done at the Pear Tree Farm, but as we built our soil's tilth, but we found we ould simply bury it. We were burying kitchen compost in designated garden areas. When you came back a few days later, you would find all kinds of insects and worms burrowing through, working to digest all the organic matter.

Meat was not included in our aerobic system because it attracted flies and created odors. Fly eggs hatch into maggots, creating more flies within 5 -15 days, with the nauseating putrescine and cadaverine odors of decay.

Here is George removing odorless finished compost for a sniff test for visitors.

NATURE FARMING

Masanobu Fukuoka is the father of no-till Nature Farming and the author of *The One-Straw Revolution*. Fukuoka rejected his training as a research scientist in plant diseases and an abandoned modern method of cultivation, dependent on heavy use of chemicals - fertilizers & insecticides, flood irrigation, mechanization, etc. He evolved his philosophy by practicing on 1 1/4 acres of rice and about 12 acres of mandarin oranges & grapefruit.

Fukuoka farmed on a hillside overlooking Matsuyama Bay across the inland sea from Hiroshima. Under his citrus, he grew radish, turnip, mustard & squash. In the mid-70s, when our friend Ellie Bluestein went to Japan, she arranged to meet with Fukuoka.

He mourned the loss of time farmers had off-season because of mechanization. He noted that they used to write poetry in the off-season. Tractors made work easier, but farmers had to work year-round to pay for them, so they had no leisure time for poetry.

He gave us other important considerations:

- *What can we NOT do that nature can do for herself?*
- *How do we work in cooperation with natural cycles?*
- *How do we minimize outside inputs and use recycled materials where possible?*
- *How do we minimize human labor?*

When Ellie visited, the winter barley had been sown directly into the field a month before, while the rice crop was still ripening. The barley was 2 or 3 inches high, green and strong. It would be stamped underfoot during the rice harvesting, but would spring back afterward. He covered it with the rice straw, which would serve as a natural mulch & compost.

Before the winter grain harvest in May, he would sow rice directly into the fields in the same manner, which he said is better than the common practice of growing it separately in flooded seed beds and then painstakingly transplanting it into muddy fields kept flooded until the rice is high. He says this old method weakens the rice and makes it more susceptible to disease and insects. Ellie saw that the grain heads were big and healthy. His fruit was sweet, juicy and insect-free and also the largest she had ever seen.

Fukuoka's book introduced us to the short Japanese hand scythe called a Kama. There was a large Japanese community of small farmers here, so we were able to find the hand tool in downtown Fresno. The serrated, curved rice blade became my favorite tool for cutting herbs.

MAIA'S HERBAL ODYSSEY

After finding a few herbal books and classes in the mid-70s, I found The California School of Herbal Studies (CSHS) in Northern California. It was run by Rosemary Gladstar, "Godmother of American Herbalism," who is a nature spirit in human form.

Rosemary gracefully expressed her immense love and appreciation for plants and all living things. Her joy at bringing green allies into her life was infectious. She wrote several books and moved to Vermont to create Sage Mountain Botanical Sanctuary, where she continues her work.

She brought in the best US & UK culinary and medicinal herbalists, and gave us wonderful book lists of other resources and other teachers.

TOURS & FOOD EXPLORING

I continued to prepare meals for our monthly House & Garden tours and other events to expose people to more wild edibles and to discuss the medicinal and digestive properties of many culinary herbs, edible flowers, and our unusual crops. After a decade of experiments, I published an herbal cookery book on CD.

I developed several herbal tea formulas that we marketed, but Flower Tea was my SunMt specialty product. A food critic from Gourmet magazine sampled it at a local restaurant and was impressed with the unique tea. He wrote an article describing George, the mountain man, clumping into the restaurant to deliver the hand-harvested organic delicacy.

Herbal Facials & Foot Baths

I also did garden facials and foot baths, where participants used my freshly harvested organic herbs and flowers in a seven-step process, working on one another. The bowls of botanical facials were then recycled into foot baths with more hot water. On the back deck, partners would massage each other's feet, working reflexology points in view of the gardens and waterfall. Lovely!

The San Francisco Chronicle said of a meal that we catered:

"*It was a book party where people nibbled at organic snacks, so in tune with the spaceship Earth ethos that some were weeds or landscaping before being recycled into canapés. Served by Maia Ballis of SunMt Research Center, they bore names like Dried Daylilies & onion dip, Tepary beans, Blue corn, & Wild Sage in whole wheat tortillas, and Chili Solar Crackers. They were washed down with Manzanita cider and an herbal Peppermint tea as bracing as a slap in the chops.*"

STRAW BALE HOUSING

In 1980-81, George was president of Rural America, a national federation of local rural community action groups, where they worked on rural housing and other rural economic issues. The final modified design for the SunMt demonstration straw bale building design SunMt took 10 years.

We started at Daniel Smith's architectural firm office on a busy Street in Berkeley. They had built a quonset hut-shaped straw bale building in the backyard. When we went inside and closed the door, all the street sounds disappeared! The comforting curved structure felt so wonderful that we were seduced. We wanted to promote low-cost, owner-builder-friendly straw-bale adobe dwellings for ourselves, farm workers, and other low-income people.

Straw Bale Project

Straw Bale bamboo pin construction class

Hay is harvested grain, but straw is the stem left behind, which is often burned, causing unhealthy levels of air particulate matter (PM2.5). When particulate matter penetrates deep into the lungs, it can increase the risk of heart disease, asthma, and low birth weight.

Air pollution in the Fresno-Madera Area is the worst in the U.S. and agricultural burning is no longer allowed. Then, using the straw for insulation would have helped reduce air pollution while providing a green insulation material.

Straw bale building was taking off in the arid Southwest. The bale walls provide superior insulation and are expected to last 200 years with owner-builder maintenance.

Straw bale construction ends up costing only about 5% less than standard construction, but its highly insulating R-30 to R-35 walls are made from a renewable waste product that can go up quickly with unskilled labor. A small group of people can build the bale walls on a weekend, so the big expense was the foundation and the roofing.

A large overhang was required to keep the building's feet dry. Natural adobe plaster was applied to the surface, unlike stucco, allowing the walls to breathe. We wanted traditional adobe floors mixed with cactus juice and waterproofed with a hemp or linseed oil topcoat as a hardening agent on the porous clay from our property.

Pest infestation remains a problem so far with the straw bale construction. An outgrowth has been the development of medium-density fiberboard composed mainly of rice straw and other grasses to sequester carbon and reduce air pollution from burning.

Sadly, after researching and designing for a decade, the cost of roofing exceeded our budget. Thanks to the generous pro bono experts, engineer Jere Mele and renowned environmental architect Arthur Dyson, who gave us an elegant, well-engineered design for the studio space we first envisioned.

Mark Lasher ended up using Mele Engineering to build a Straw Bale wall for his downtown Fresno house. We modified the first experimental Dyson design when we decided it would be our retirement dwelling. The unused project plans were donated to Paul Chavez at the Cesar Chavez Foundation to help them provide owner-builder farmworker housing.

Dakota Eco Garden

Architect Arthur Dyson used a demonstration straw bale back wall for insulation for one of the small structures he designed for Dakota EcoGarden. Their effective program accepts unhoused people who need a boost to re-enter the workforce within a few months and supports that goal. The main house has the shared utilities for cooking, bathing and washing clothes, but six people have small outdoor private shelters in various experimental designs by Arthur Dyson.

Owner Nancy Waidtlow was awarded the distinguished Mr. Rodgers Good Neighbor award in 2021, and the Fresno City Council named Aug. 10, 2023, Dakota EcoGarden Day in Fresno. Her non-profit's small but successful efforts give each resident the educational, emotional, and physical tools, caring support, and training to efficiently help end their homelessness.

Embodied Energy

Working on Straw Bale Building research, we became more aware of "embodied energy" - how much energy it takes to produce the materials that we use in construction. But it also applies to everything we use, and it made me consider the energy used to produce all the things I use. I consider durability and lifespan for purchases. It would be helpful to include carbon footprint on product labeling, as we do for nutritional content in packaged foods.

Chapter Four
GREEN AGRICULTURE

Agriculture & Landfills The related areas of agriculture and landfills are where some of the most effective, least expensive current and emerging options can have a significant impact on climate change mitigation. Expanding composting of biomass from agriculture, forests and landfills, and applying the finished compost to farms and rangeland can dramatically reduce greenhouse gas (GHG) emissions and sequester carbon.

It is one important tool among many needed to combat climate change. A 2014 study suggested that covering 5% of California's rangelands alone could capture an amount of carbon roughly equal to all the state's residential and commercial emissions.

CARBON FARMING

The Marin Carbon Farming Project was created by California rancher John Wick. He is a pioneer of carbon farming and a leading promoter of compost for sequestering carbon in the soil. Through his work with the Marin Carbon Project, he has demonstrated that applying a thin layer of compost to rangelands can significantly increase forage production, enhance soil health, and draw down atmospheric carbon dioxide into the soil. Land-management practices are one of the few affordable options available today for drawing down carbon into the earth's surface, making it a huge carbon sponge.

The Carbon Cycle: the continuous movement of carbon atoms between the atmosphere, oceans, land, and living organisms. Burning fossil fuels for energy rapidly releases carbon stored underground for millions of years. This excess carbon in the atmosphere contributes to climate change. Carbon farming slows the release of carbon back into the atmosphere through composting, ensuring that the carbon leaving an ecosystem is less than the carbon entering it. As animals and plants die, they decompose, releasing carbon back into the atmosphere unless it is sequestered in the soil.

Community Composting

Community Composting has been supported by California Government to divert biological residues from landfills at the community level, while producing rich compost as an input for more local food self-reliance in low-income food deserts.

Local residents brought their biodegradable waste to a composting site, where they could return for finished compost, allowing them to grow some of their own food. By prioritizing composting, we could potentially produce up to 12 million tons of soil amendments each year, which are needed to meet our goals of carbon sequestration, food security, and climate resilience.

REGENERATIVE AGRICULTURE

Regenerative Agriculture incorporates carbon farming and seeks to improve and rehabilitate the health and biodiversity of farming ecosystems. It aims to regenerate soil health, increase biodiversity, improve the water cycle and increase ecosystem resilience using practices listed below:

1. No-till or Minimum Tillage: helps retain soil structure, moisture, and beneficial soil organisms.

2. Cover Crops: help protect the soil from erosion, suppress weeds, improve soil structure, add organic matter, and enhance biodiversity.

3. Crop Rotation: helps to break pest and disease cycles, improve soil health, and maintain nutrient balance in the soil.

4. Adding Compost and Organic Matter: enhances soil fertility, improves water retention, promotes beneficial microbial activity, and reduces the need for synthetic inputs. Adding Humisoil® to Regenerative Agroecology practices could be a great benefit.

5. Integrated Pest Management: uses natural predators, diverse crop rotations, and healthy soils to manage pests and diseases and reduces reliance on chemical inputs.

6. Agroforestry: introduces trees and shrubs into agricultural landscapes to help improve biodiversity, provide habitat for beneficial organisms, enhance soil health, and regulate microclimates.

7. Water Management: using water harvesting, efficient irrigation systems, and contour farming helps conserve water and reduce soil erosion.

8. Livestock Integration: livestock integrated into cropping systems through practices like rotational grazing can improve soil health, nutrient cycling, and farm productivity.

9. Holistic Management: considers the farm as a whole system focused on long-term sustainability and resilience.

Benefits of Compost

California's Central Valley Regenerative Growers promote practices like cover cropping, no-till, and integrated livestock in almond and other systems. Just a 1% increase in soil organic matter increases water storage potential on an acre by more than 20,000 gallons. They have used a 3% increase in compost, which increases water storage potential per acre by 3.5%. With a mix of three types of cover crops with different root structures:

- brassicas,
- legumes grasses.

Crops are mowed, leaving the above-ground biomass and the root structure below the soil surface. Seeds are drilled in rows, or the green manure is grown between trees. Water-holding capacity makes the soil and plants more resistant to drought and increases biodiversity both above and below the soil surface, reducing irrigation needs while increasing sequestration of climate-damaging CO2.

By the third year, with 3% added organic matter, the soil yields more nutrient-dense food with less irrigation while building soil. The US is losing soil 10 times faster than it is replenished. These regenerative soil practices convert our working lands from net carbon emitters to carbon sinks.

Composting in the US

The US currently has a recycling and composting rate of 32%. In California, biomass is composted at 166 permitted composting facilities, both at large-scale commercial facilities and through decentralized community and on-farm operations creating nutrient-rich soil amendments for agriculture, rangelands and public landscaping. But the effort is not yet 100% for complex reasons. As one composting enthusiast puts it, "It's only waste if you waste it," and VRM's continuous fermentation composting system is an exponential leap in composting technology.

VRM HUMISOIL®

HumiSoil® was developed by Australian entrepreneur Ken Bellamy, founder of VRM BioLogik®. It is an advanced composting method that enhances soil health in a unique way. Because it produces water as a byproduct, his groundbreaking composting technique can quickly restore soil, creating more resilient, higher-yielding, nutrient-rich crops.

It can even grow crops like potatoes in desert sand and has restored drought-devastated rangeland. That land is now suitable for grazing cattle, receiving rainfall for only one month a year with no supplemental irrigation. This system can also turn dairy manure into a low-odor, high-quality soil amendment that improves soil fertility, thanks to the moisture it produces.

See the YouTube video on the United Nations Conference on Climate Change: VRM at UNCCD COP16 2024. It shows side-by-side soil and crops in the Middle East and China that you have to see to believe. Watch an amazed worker pulling a potato out of the sand!

VRM BioLogik® HumiSoil® is an advanced anaerobic (no oxygen) composting system that eliminates the need for physically turning piles, reducing labor, equipment costs and carbon emissions while it captures and retains nutrients, carbon, and supports specific soil microbes that generate water, acting as a water reservoir, unlike regular humus, which primarily stores existing water.

This process converts waste into a valuable product rich in humus and microbial activity, thereby improving soil health, better water management, and increasing crop yields for end-users. The system accelerates the natural process of humus formation, turning waste into a valuable, nutrient-rich soil enhancer in 6 months, rather than the 1 year it takes for unturned standard compost.

LANDFILLS: Garbage Into Gold

Since 2022, Californians have been required to separate organic materials into green bins, which are then diverted from landfills for processing into compost, mulch, and various liquid, gas, and solid biofuels. Current legislation allows on-site composting of larger volumes of agricultural waste for farms to community-level operations without complicated permitting. It also allows growers to sell or give away larger amounts of finished compost to help meet the state's organic waste diversion goals.

Using the VRM HumiSoil composting system could allow growers and landfill owners to use this green "waste" to produce a higher-value finished compost, which would have greater market value while more rapidly rebuilding our soils. This solution could become a major building block towards a regenerative bioeconomy. Even if you don't believe in climate change, building local self-reliance is an undeniably good idea.

Food Security

The alarming loss of billions of tons of U.S. soil annually threatens our food supply, but HumiSoil's properties enable the cultivation of high-demand crops, such as potatoes and heavy-feeding onions, in sand! The system is already used and produced in China, Africa, the Middle East, and in Florida and Texas in the U.S. Because humus sequesters ozone and carbon, experts forecast widespread implementation in rangelands could sequester enough of both to mitigate climate change impacts.

Another YouTube Humisoil video shows a Chinese trial (with English subtitles) featuring a worker remarking on the pest resistance of a VRM tomato plant, its large size, and its "real" tomato flavor. During the COVID-19 pandemic, people who couldn't leave their homes were able to grow high-nutrient foods in their yards in China, Singapore, and Indonesia using HumiSoil®, creating a more nutrient-dense, secure food supply.

How It Works

To activate their process, VRM uses a proprietary fertilizer, which they spray onto an 8 ft. high compost pile with an ingenious "M"- shaped top. Then they tarp the pile to prevent moisture evaporation and provide the conditions, minerals and nutrients

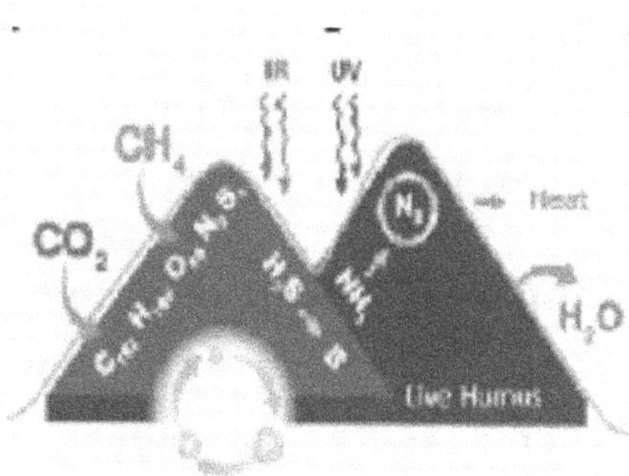

needed for the process. Diverse microbes in the soil begin to rise and move along the top surface, guided by the "M"- shaped pile form, following a pathway of nutrients in water created by chemical reactions, in an infinity sign of perpetual motion.

That movement delivers the required nutrients for soil building, eliminating the need to physically turn the piles required for standard composting, which is a huge savings in labor, energy, and equipment costs.

Over 6 month's time, that process creates high-quality humus. Humus is the nutrient-rich, dark part of the soil structure, a crucial habitat for diverse microorganisms that enhance soil fertility, structure, and water retention.

HumiSoil® Benefits:

These features make VRM HumiSoil® composting a more effective and sustainable option.

Greenhouse Gas (GHG) Sequestration: Both standard and VRM HumiSoil® composting systems capture carbon from the atmosphere, contributing to climate change; but while standard composting can ideally lower methane emissions by 39%–84% more than landfills, HumiSoil® produces none. Experts believe that widespread adoption of this low-tech solution could substantially reduce carbon emissions while improving soil health and food quality.

Rapid Soil Regeneration: HumiSoil® composting can rebuild soil health in as little as 6 months. Although some benefits are visible sooner with conventional composting methods, it may take years and far larger quantities to show significant improvements in soil health.

Efficiency: Standard composting requires a balance of material types, water, and starter compost, which needs to be physically turned to add oxygen for proper breakdown. VRM's system requires one application of their liquid activator; the pile is covered for six months without further input or machinery required to turn it.

Water Production: making VRM HumiSoil® uniquely produces water as a byproduct, enhancing soil moisture retention and aiding plant growth, particularly in arid regions.

Resilience to Environmental Stress: HumiSoil® can improve soil fertility across various environments. The resulting soil treated with finished HumiSoil® is more resilient to drought, salinity, pests, high heat and other stressors, making it adaptable for different agricultural needs.

Enhanced Nutrient Availability: HumiSoil composting focuses on creating nutrient-rich humus, which improves the availability of essential nutrients for plants. The enhanced soil structure supports better aeration, drainage, and root development, leading to healthier plants. This method promotes a diverse and active microbial community in the soil, which is crucial for nutrient cycling and soil fertility.

Higher Crop Quality: Trials indicate that crops grown in HumiSoil are more resilient, grow larger and tend to have superior taste compared to those grown in standard compost.

Odor Control: HumiSoil composting can convert smelly manure and organic waste into low-odor, high-value soil amendments.

Sustainable Waste Management: VRM HumiSoil® composting turns agricultural waste and other biological materials into valuable resources, reducing the amount of waste sent to landfills.

Better Orchard Management: The U.S. faces significant soil loss, endangering food supplies. Transforming biological waste into HumiSoil® presents a better alternative to burying retired orchard wood, which depletes soil nitrogen.

Whole Orchard Recycling: California has reduced air pollution by banning the burning of retired orchard wood, but Whole Orchard Recycling (WOR) involves grinding whole trees into wood chips, and then turning them into the soil before replanting orchards after one year. But all that carbon is released over time, tying up necessary nitrogen and nutrients, making them unavailable for future crops. Standard composting or VRM's Continuous Fermentation Composting is a better solution.

Unlike expensive, high-tech carbon-sequestering proposals that do just one thing, VRM's continuous fermentation composting produces carbon sequestration and high-quality soil amendment that create ongoing moisture and fertility. It is the most exciting low-cost, low-tech, multi-benefit soil solution for sequestering carbon to mitigate climate change that I have found.

COST-BENEFIT of CARBON CAPTURE SYSTEMS

Compare the benefits of using VRM's Humisoil® process over other carbon drawdown options:

Direct air carbon capture and storage technology is expensive, **costing around $500-$1,000 per metric ton of stored carbon dioxide, but offers no other benefits.** This is an illogical waste of resources.

Standard & Industrial Composting: using standard aerobic composting **costs about $100 per ton** and **requires 5-14 tons per acre.**

VRM Biologik HumiSoil® is an advanced anaerobic composting system that eliminates the need for physically turning piles. Depending on the material price and the amount used, it costs 77% to 95% less than standard compost but requires **only 1-2 tons per acre.**

Landfill Composting: advanced composting of biomass from green bins has the potential to solve most of our landfill issues. If we require all plastics to be recyclable, renewable bioplastics, and efficiently divert hazardous waste.

The retail price for processed HumiSoil® depends on the quality and quantity. High-value compost can become a marketable soil amendment, turning garbage into gold. Current HumiSoil® prices in Texas range from $10 to $55 per cubic yard, depending on quality. 40 lb. bags of high-quality HumiSoil® can retail for over $100, creating an income stream from excess supply.

See: VRM Contact: www.vrmbiologik.com/

Chemical Impacts on Human Health

There are three classes of pesticides widely used in agriculture and pest control:

- Organophosphates (OPs),
- Organochlorines (OCs), and
- Pyrethroids (PYRs).

The collective impacts of cumulative exposure to these chemicals can include neurodevelopmental risks, carcinogenic potential, endocrine disruption, immune system impacts, and environmental impacts on our food supply.

Cancer is caused by genetic mutations internally, but external factors like tobacco, radiation, poor diet and environmental pollutants can damage the body's innate ability to control cell growth.

Chemical Agriculture Risks

The California Department of Pesticide Regulation data shows the record high in California of 215 million pounds came in 1998 which was reduced to 209 million pounds of pesticides in 2016. Safety advocates point to the danger of continuing reliance on dangerous chemicals.

Communities in rural agricultural and suburban communities near agriculture and hazardous chemicals, people are breathing, drinking, and eating small amounts of pesticides daily. From: *Ag Chemical toxicology from American chemical Society © ACS 2021 study*

MUSHROOMS - MYCOREMEDIATION

Paul Stamets invented mycoremediation, a form of bioremediation in which fungi are used to remove a wide array of contaminants from damaged environments or wastewater. It can be used in soil contaminated with petroleum or diesel oil, as demonstrated in a 2005 remediation experiment in which four soil piles were contaminated with diesel at a concentration of polycyclic aromatic hydrocarbons (PAHs) of 10,000 ppm.

One pile was treated with enzymes, one with bacteria, one with oyster mushroom mycelium, and one was untreated as a control. After six weeks, three of the piles showed no improvement, while the pile treated with mycelium was covered in hundreds of pounds of healthy mushrooms! The mycelium of oyster mushrooms produces enzymes that break hydrogen-carbon bonds that hold hydrocarbons together, and it obtains a lot of nutrition in the process.

Fungi (Mushrooms) have been proven to be a cheap, effective and environmentally sound way to transform contaminants, include heavy metals, organic pollutants, textile dyes, leather tanning chemicals and wastewater, petroleum fuels, polycyclic aromatic hydrocarbons, pharmaceuticals and personal care products, pesticides and herbicides in land, fresh water, and marine environments. The byproducts of the remediation can be valuable materials themselves, such as edible or medicinal mushrooms and laccase enzyme, making the remediation process profitable.

My daughter Victoria and her husband grew Paul Stamet's Fungi Perfecti shiitake mushrooms for the medicinal market. I continue to be dazzled by Stamet's research and revelations about the beneficial relationship between humans and fungi, and I have benefited from his Fungi Perfecti Host Defense® immune support formula.

Biochar Soil Amendment

Biochar is a charcoal-like substance made from woody biomass. It is rich in carbon, highly porous, and stable. Used as a soil amendment, it can sequester carbon for thousands of years while enhancing soil fertility and structure, improving water retention, and increasing crop yields. It can reduce GHG emissions associated with conventional agricultural practices: methane (CH_4) and nitrous oxide (N_2O).

HUMANS & TREES

Trees are the biggest lungs of the planet. They use photosynthesis to produce energy from sunlight, releasing oxygen, while the human body inhales the needed oxygen and releases carbon dioxide, which the trees need so they can release oxygen in a perfect symbiotic loop.

Trees provide numerous environmental benefits, supporting rich biodiversity by offering food and shelter for countless species, improving soil health, and conserving water through reduced runoff. They help cool urban areas by providing shade and can lower air temperatures through evapotranspiration, which reduces the need for air conditioning.

They are crucial for climate regulation by sequestering large amounts of carbon dioxide, improving air quality through photosynthesis and pollutant absorption, and trapping particulate matter on their leaves.

Trees are an important part of the web of life. A study by K. Matsunaga, a marine biologist at Hokkaido University in Japan, showed how fallen leaves from trees leach acids carrying iron into streams and rivers, which are carried to the ocean where they fuel plankton, the first link in the food chain.

They planted more trees along Japan's coastline, and the number of fish and oysters available for local harvest increased over time. Since the 1980s, the Japanese have practiced "Forest Bathing," a healing practice that involves walking in the oxygen-rich forest atmosphere and inhaling the medicinal essential oils exuded by trees. On walks around my apartment complex, I inhale the aroma as I pass under a row of redwoods, where I mentally thank them for the oxygen that they produce and, in return, give them the gift of my exhaled CO2 that they need - better than hugging a tree.

MegaFlora® THE MOST AMAZING TREE

Left to right: 5 year-old MegaFlora 65 ft., 4-year flowering tree, 5 Year tree leaf size Photo of flowering trees courtesy Genesis Agroforestry

All trees are engaged in helping to regulate global gases and climate patterns, but one is exceptional. MegaFlora® is Genesis Agroforestry's brand name for their proprietary, non-

GMO trihybrid from a cross of three Paulownia species and a hardwood. The result is a slightly faster-growing, stronger Paulownia tree, with all the other properties that make it a highly valuable resource. It was developed in the 1990s by head scientist Dr. Ray Allen, who holds an exclusive worldwide license to the proprietary method and process for creating this amazing tree.

Megaflora vs Paulownia Properties

To harvest for lumber, MegaFlora® trees may take 7 to 9 years to fully mature. For additional revenue and biodiversity, annual field crops may be grown as an intercrop in the open space between the rows or under their canopies, depending on the crop. The best options are shade-tolerant plants like mint, chives, lettuce, parsley and spinach are candidates. The mother-of-pearl tree (Paulowniaceae) is native to Central and Western China and is the fastest-growing tree in the world.

The main problems with these trees are their invasive nature from prolific seeding and vigorous root suckers, weak, brittle wood prone to storm damage, and susceptibility to insect infestation. Paulownia has antiviral leaves, flowers, and bark, used in China for foot-and-mouth disease and other illnesses. The MegaFlora® tree has been bred to be seed-sterile, so it is not invasive and has none of Paulownia's problems, but may share Paulownia's beneficial antiviral property.

Features of Megaflora®:

Fast growing but non-invasive: the fastest growing tree in the world - Can grow 30 feet in 3 years and up to 82 feet high.

Lightweight strength: Equal strength to pine but weighs half as much.

Carbon sequestration: Multiple universities, including the University of California, Davis, have rated it the best tree for carbon sequestration. Dr Allen said the University of Beijing, China, rated it 4 times better than their own species of Paulownia at removing carbon from the air while releasing 4 times the oxygen, a benefit to their poor air quality. They also conducted research on using the trees to remove heavy metals in a mining area, with positive results.

High nitrogen leaves: a large leafed perennial equivalent to annual alfalfa for animal feed.

Coppices: It regrows from the cut stump 3-4 times.

Climate limits: the tree grows in extreme climates and is resistant to physical stressors.

Low water use: 2-3 gallons per day per tree the 1st year, then drip irrigation overnight once a week or less. More water grows larger leaves.

Soil types: The tree can be grown on marginal land, leaving prime soil to grow crops that require it. MegaFlora® plantations have been grown in the Gobi Desert of Mongolia.

Fixes nitrogen in the soil: Nitrogen is crucial for plant growth, as it plays a key role in producing proteins, amino acids, and chlorophyll. It is essential for processes such as photosynthesis and cell division, for vigorous foliage, root development, and overall yield.

Bee Food: Beautiful purple and white high-nectar-producing flowers bloom 4-6 weeks in spring for honey production. Honey naturally has antibacterial properties and the honey from these flowers may also contain the antiviral properties of the flowers as well.

Animal feed: The large leaves and flowers have protein content similar to that of alfalfa.

High insect resistance due to the absence of sap under the bark.

High-quality wood: Lightweight yet strong lumber with excellent fiber for paper production.

Deep root system: It grows roots 30 ft. deep and 3 times broader than the canopy, reinforcing the soil mass and holding it together against the forces of wind and water.

Produces high-energy fuel: The wood burns 8,400 BTU vs. 7,200 for conifer wood.

Intercropping: Where there is open ground between rows of trees, crops like peppers, tomatoes, squash, soybeans, or grains can be grown in the sun between the trees, while shade-tolerant greens like lettuce, arugula, spinach, and kale may grow under the canopy for protection in hot climates. Intercropping has the dual benefit of additional income and biodiversity.

Commercial Uses:

Reforestation projects: reforesting a deforested area.

Fast maturity: harvest for biomass or lumber in 3-7 years, compared to 20-25 years for pine. Pine trees take 30-40 years to fully mature, but MegaFlora fully matures in 10 years.

Side limbs and tree tops may be removed in three years to produce biofuels, biochar, or renewable graphene, leaving the main tree to grow larger for higher-value lumber.

Fire break: The wood has excellent flame-retardant properties, as it ignites at 788°F vs. 446°F for conifers.

Afforestation projects – planting a new forest.

Commercial plantations or woodlots – biomass or wood chips for renewable energy generation, or milling high-quality wood products.

Environmental remediation – removal of hazardous inorganic chemicals from soil and water at closed mines or abandoned industrial sites.

Wildfire remediation: its deep-penetrating roots are effective at stabilizing soil and reducing erosion and improving soil and water quality

Bioeconomy Jobs: Dr. Ray Allen created 60,000 jobs in remote rural areas of China, plus 3,000 permanent greenhouse jobs over 8 years of developing plantations there.

Genesis Agroforestry has planted over 15 million trees in over 15 countries. They can provide root cuttings for large commercial-scale propagation and are interested in working with contract plantation growers of their trees.

Contact: brad@genesisagroforestry.com

Future Forests?

Our government views forests as a natural resource to be extracted for profit, so the Forestry Department is under the Department of Agriculture because our forests are managed as a crop. In 2023, the United States exported approximately 9.8 billion in wood products, mainly to Canada, China, and the United Kingdom. In 2024, the US imported 23.8 billion in wood products, mostly from Canada, to meet residential construction demand that we cannot supply.

Rethinking Forest Management

Independent forester, Chris Welter, had a small company decade ago that approached timber harvest as "gardening" the forest. He selectively harvested trees for sustainability and fire resistance, using equipment that did not compress the soil. His thoughtful approach could not survive then in competition with companies that had contracts with the Forest Service (USFS) to clear-cut.

With less pressure to harvest forests for wood products, his techniques could set a new standard for Forest Service timber contracts and also enhance fire management. More recently, the Forest Service recognizes and honors Indigenous stewardship and sovereignty, and actively includes Indigenous tribes in management decisions through formal consultation, co-stewardship, and dedicated Tribal Relations programs.

Federal directives and action plans strengthen nation-to-nation relationships and incorporate tribal values into land management. This includes mechanical thinning to reduce the number of trees and create strategically placed fuel breaks to slow or stop fire spread. These efforts are part of a larger state-led initiative to improve forest health and fire resilience, such as frequent, low-intensity "cultural burns."

Bio-diverse Plantations?

The Central Valley of California is crucial to US agriculture because it has been one of the most productive agricultural regions in the country. Using less than 1% of its farmland, it supplies 8% of the nation's food. It is currently the leading dairy producer and provides a substantial amount of its beef and produces 40% of all fruits, nuts, and vegetables grown in the US.

The Westlands Water District has about 600,000 acres of farmland, with about 568,000 acres irrigable. Over 100,000 acres of impaired land have been acquired by the district and retired from farming since 2002. Some of this retired land is now being used for solar farms.

VRM Humisoil® & Megaflora® Trees?

Imagine a trial on some of the soils in the retired 100,000 acres that have poor drainage and salinity problems of this one agricultural area treated with VRM HumiSoil®. Then, 300 trees per acre were planted, with field crops grown between the rows. Every 1,000 acres could hold 300,000 trees, demonstrating how to use marginal land!

Some wood from side limbs, tops, or whole trees could be harvested for biogas fuel within 3 years, yielding up to 150 tons per acre per year. Some trees could be harvested for wood products in 5 years and others in an optimal 9 years.

MegaFlora® plantations once cut to the stump, will regrow 3 to 4 times. They can be harvested in a minimum of 3 years but are best harvested in rotations of 5 to 7 years. That can generate approximately 85,000-128,000 board feet of dimensional lumber per acre. An average 1,000 square-foot two-bedroom home requires about 8,000 to 11,000 board feet of lumber, so one acre of trees is enough to build about 12 homes every 3- 5 years. A three-year-old tree can sequester a ton of carbon until harvested, and the leaves can be harvested annually for animal feed!

Aquaculture

Agriculture is the growing of crops in soil, while Aquaculture is the farming of aquatic fish, shellfish and seaweeds. Seaweed is packed with vitamins, minerals (like iodine, calcium), fiber, and antioxidants. It's low in calories and high in fiber, supporting gut health, and Japanese people have unique gut bacteria to help digest its complex sugars.

Kombu (kelp) is rich in glutamic acid, the source of umami. Umami is the fifth basic taste in Japanese cuisine, alongside sweet, sour, salty, and bitter, and translates as "pleasant savory taste." Different types like kombu, wakame, and nori are used in soups, salads, wraps (nori), and as flavoring agents, adding depth to dishes.

Red seaweed used in cattle feed can reduce their methane emissions by up to 98% in feedlots and by 37.7% in grazing beef cattle. Studies noted no negative impact on milk production or animal health. It uses excess nutrients, absorbs CO2, enhances coastal resilience, and provides sustainable food and feed, with the potential for large-scale carbon sequestration as farms adapt to changing conditions.

While specific challenges exist, its fundamental benefits position it as a key part of the solution for coastal communities facing climate impacts. Currently, aquaculture is the sustainable method for producing the seaweed needed for this purpose, as harvesting wild seaweed is unsustainable.

Aquaculture is growing to meet the demand for this feed, with new large-scale farms being built and significant investment in the industry. But the vast amounts needed globally remain a challenge. Lab-grown versions of the active enzyme are also being researched to meet the global demand.

Urban Hydroponics

Instead of soil, Hydroponics uses a carefully balanced, water-based solution containing all necessary macro and micronutrients plants need. Commonly used for lettuce, herbs, peppers, tomatoes and cucumbers. It uses up to 90% less water and enables space-saving, dense vertical planting for year-round high yields. The urban hydroponic system is popular in the Asia Pacific, the Netherlands and North America. Legalization of cannabis in some countries has boosted demand.

Hydroponic systems powered by fossil fuels can have a higher carbon footprint than traditional methods. Renewable energy is crucial for a positive impact. Plants naturally absorb CO2, and hydroponics optimizes this by growing more food in less space. Its biggest climate advantage comes from replacing conventional farming's carbon footprint by cutting rural to urban transport emissions, minimizing land use, and reducing reliance on carbon-intensive soil tilling. Hydroponics can also grow saplings faster for reforestation projects, speeding up carbon capture.

Challenges include high startup costs and the need for specialized supplies, high energy use, and technical expertise. There is reduced soil-borne disease, but it allows rapid spread of waterborne diseases, and there are pest management issues, all requiring constant monitoring, plus vulnerability to power outages. There are environmental concerns over the disposal of used nutrient solutions. There are also limitations for crops such as root vegetables and tall crops.

Edible Insects

Edible insects are legally permissible and increasingly available in the U.S. They are generally regarded as safe (GRAS), relying on industry self-regulation. Edible ants, beetles, caterpillars, wasps, bees, crickets, locusts, and grasshoppers are consumed roasted, fried, or ground into flour for snacks and protein boosts.

Beetles (Coleoptera) are the most consumed order, while crickets and mealworms are the leading farmed insects for human food. Live and dried mealworms are sold as pet food, wild bird feed and fishing bait. People with crustacean allergies should avoid it because it contains proteins similar to those in crustaceans, and there is a high risk of allergic reactions.

Grasshoppers are high in protein, vitamins, and minerals, and are low in calories. Grasshoppers in Mexico, known as Chapulines, are seasoned with garlic, lime, & chili and are a staple, eaten in tacos, on guacamole, or as snacks. They are also popular in Africa and Asia, often fried, roasted, or seasoned as strcct food.

Chapter Five
FUTURE WATER

Before you complain about rainy days, remember that water is essential for all forms of life on Earth, serving as a fundamental resource that sustains biological processes and ecosystems. Moreover, water is vital for agriculture, supporting crop growth and food production that sustains human populations. It serves as a medium for transportation, energy generation, and industrial processes, while also supporting the health of aquatic ecosystems and enabling economic development, human health, and overall environmental well-being.

Did you know:

- Almost 97% of the world's water is salty or undrinkable.
- Another 2% is locked in ice caps and glaciers, leaving 1% for all of humanity's needs, municipal, agricultural, and industrial.
- Water regulates the temperature of Earth and the human body, carrying nutrients and oxygen to our cells, cushions joints, protects organs and tissues and removes wastes.
- 75% of a living tree and the human brain is water.
- A person can live about a month without food, but only about a week without water.

- Water is deeply connected to our environment. What we pour on the ground or spew into the sky ends up in our water.
- The average U.S. Household water use totals about 50 gallons per person per day.
- The average cost for water supplied to a home in the U.S is about 2 dollars per 100 gallons, or 1 penny per 5 gallons.
- Water expands by 9% when it freezes, forming ice, which is why ice floats in water.

Fun Facts circulated by the water committee, Women's International League for Peace & Freedom

Microplastics

Water quality is essential to human health. Microplastics are environmental pollutants that prevail in the oceans, remote islands, and polar regions. Exposure to microplastics presents a major emerging threat to ecosystems due to their potential adverse effects. Toxic effects may vary, but studies have found microplastics in the human body, including the arteries, placenta, organs, and brain. Research suggests they can trigger cell damage and gene changes. Reduce intake by avoiding plastic cookware and choosing natural fiber clothing over synthetic fiber.

Filters That Remove Microplastics

Generally, reverse osmosis (RO) systems can remove microplastics. The best ones have multi-stage purification and remineralization: the Waterdrop G3P600 8-stage tankless reverse osmosis and the smart LED faucet are currently top-rated. RO countertop products require no plumbing.: Aquatru.

Berkey is a countertop system that can remove microplastics, but does retain minerals, is lower cost, and is portable with no water waste. The specific test for microplastics has not been performed but microplastics are typically found in water. 2.5 Microns (2,500 nanometers).

Black Berkey elements filter down to 24-26 nanometers, much smaller than the size of microplastics. Berkey can also remove "forever chemicals" PFAS, PFOS, and PFHxS to 99.09%. Their filters use gravity-fed microfiltration and activated carbon media. The carbon block is effective at adsorbing many contaminants, including certain microplastics. They also filter out 99.9% of a wide range of pesticides and herbicides, including glyphosate, atrazine, DDT and more, but not all chemicals. Berkey® PF-2™ filters remove up to 99.75% of fluoride and target full arsenic removal.

PUR PLUS pitcher and faucet filters are certified by NSF to reduce microplastics and lead, which Brita does not remove. Some PUR pitcher filters do not have this certification. Brita is often preferred for faster filtration and better-tasting water at a lower cost, thanks to its cheaper filters.

Is Water A Human Right?

In 2012, Governor Jerry Brown signed a bill making California the first state to declare that everyone has a right to clean, safe, and affordable water. A decade later, the permissive language allows water contracts to "consider" this mandate, and the many water district jurisdictions under contract make it difficult for community organizations trying to help people access available funds.

Even though they pay high water bills, many small rural areas have only tainted tap water for domestic use. They face the problem of getting the water district to cooperate, a challenge made more difficult during drought, when rates increased 154% in 2023, until the communities fought back.

Irrigators pay far less for agricultural use for complicated reasons, including costly infrastructure investments and slow planning. Short-term State help of bottled and hauled water only prevents disaster and is not a long-term solution. I suggested that the 400-household community might create an entity to purchase in bulk and sell at wholesale to individual Berkey water filtration system buyers. Depending on water quality, the filters can last five years.

That idea did not work then. Emerging Renewable Graphene technology may reduce prices, making individual filtration affordable if offered on time payments. Meanwhile, subsidence (land sinking from excess water extraction) continues to threaten access to even low-quality water. A major agricultural producer research shows that Fresno's drinking water has PFAS "forever chemicals" at over 600% above EPA safe limits, in addition to PFOS and PFHxS at the highest rates found.

About 75% of US drinking water is disinfected with chlorine, which depresses thyroid function. People with Hashimoto's thyroiditis autoimmune issues may be negatively impacted.

FUTURE WATER

Water conservation is the easiest, cheapest and best choice. If we stop thinking of the flush toilet and kitchen drain as places to dispose of material that can better be processed in soil, we can help preserve this precious resource. Graywater from showers, sinks, and washing machines can be used for landscape irrigation and toilet and urinal flushing after treatment. For irrigation use, it's best to use biodegradable, plant-friendly dishwashing and bath soaps. Avoid powdered detergents with high salt or boron content.

Recycled Gray Water Gray water from kitchen and bath faucets can be filtered and reused for irrigation in Israel. California, Arizona, Colorado, Florida, Texas, and Hawaii are considering this option and developing guidelines. It is a common practice in rural areas. Gravity-fed, untreated systems used for sub-surface irrigation are simple to install and maintain, but higher-quality water from treated systems allows gray water to be used for toilet flushing.

Water Scarcity Agriculture uses 80% of the Colorado River's water, shared by about 40 entities in the U.S. and Mexico. Arizona is seeing agricultural land retired from production due to water scarcity. Less energy-intensive has no environmental hazards. Use of Humisoil has the potential to bring some land back into production.

DESALINATION

Desalination technology, which costs $9 per 1,000 gallons, has dropped to $2 - $5. But California's Central Valley is landlocked. Sea level rise driven by climate change will eventually cause saltwater intrusion from San Francisco Bay into the Sacramento Delta. During droughts, when river flows are insufficient to flush saltwater back into the ocean, it can contaminate the Central Valley irrigation canals.

Desalination successes in Israel and Catalina Island off the California Coast have created the illusion of a "silver bullet" solution. Desalination can be done, but plants are costly to operate, require enormous amounts of energy, and have had negative environmental impacts from the greenhouse gas emissions produced during operation. New generation designs offer better solutions.

Desalination Challenges

There are brine issues from the concentrated salt, which is standardly disposed of back into the ocean. That can raise seawater salinity enough to damage local marine ecosystems and water quality. Brine can also contain toxic metals, as well as pesticides and acids. Research continues on the possible use of brine in concrete, but it is naturally prone to moisture absorption, susceptible to wind- and water-driven erosion, and can cause corrosion of metal components used in construction. More creative, greener solutions are required. Graphene films are revolutionizing desalination filtration , offering superior antifouling properties and chemical stability and promising cheaper, smaller, and more sustainable water purification systems, though large-scale manufacturing challenges remain.

Current desalination uses energy-intensive, advanced reverse osmosis, which forces seawater through semi-permeable membranes under high pressure to separate salt and impurities from the water. The best systems our powered by solar energy. Reverse osmosis can remove beneficial minerals, causing magnesium deficiencies in humans and agriculture unless they are added after filtration.

The discharge of highly salty brine back into the sea is a concern for marine ecosystems. 1 gallon of filtered seawater = 1 pound of salt. *See Emerging technology in Chapter 9 about emerging sodium-ion battery technology*

HIGH-TECH WATER HARVESTING

Hydropanels: Inventor Cody Friesen's company, Zero Mass Water, uses solar panels that produce water rather than electricity, with no additional power source. They work in arid desert regions like Arizona to soggy, overcast areas like the Pacific Northwest.

Each expensive $3,000 Hydropanel can reliably deliver an average of 1.3 gallons (3-5 liters) of water a day over a 15-year lifespan. Multiple panels provide Friesen's family of four humans and two dogs with pure water for drinking and cooking in arid Arizona.

Metal-Organic Frameworks (MOFs): are porous metal clusters linked by organic molecules, utilized in hi-tech solar-powered atmospheric water-harvesting units. They extracted water vapor from desert air in a minute and produced a cup of water in a day.

The components are highly durable and can be recycled sustainably with zero discharges at $3 for 2.2 lbs. of water (1 kilogram), depending on relative humidity. The minimum is 10% humidity. The creators won the 2025 Nobel Prize in Chemistry for this new class of materials with immense potential in energy and the environment, like carbon dioxide capture & hydrogen storage, and also diverse health care applications.

LOW TECH WATER

Paleolithic Rivers: The California Department of Water Resources has been using a high-tech Light Detection and Ranging (LIDAR) airborne survey to help find Paleolithic River channels. The laser light system is mounted on helicopters or drones that send pulses of electromagnetic signals to create intricate three-dimensional maps in several ways.

The technique was piloted in California by Stanford Professor Rosemary Knight in the Sierra foothills and the East Side Central Valley.

The new mapping technology can indicate Paleolithic River beds, invisible on the surface, by tracking changes in river beds over thousands of years. They can now identify old riverbed sites with deposits of large to small gravel and rocks, allowing more underwater recharge during years of high runoff.

Humisoil's Hydrosynthesis

Hydrosynthesis means the ability not just to retain, but to create water through a chemical reaction. A United Nations climate change summit in Arabia documented the VRM process tested in Jordan, where they measured water usage by comparing irrigated sand plots with HumiSoil-treated sand. Side-by-side measurements showed that HumiSoil increased soil water content by 9,068 gallons per acre per day in the top 19 inches in the essential root zone where plants feed. That is enough to support the crop and buffer crops against desert droughts.

They used an ancient, high-yield annual wheat variety already adapted to the climate. Then the crop amazingly grew the next year without replanting. It actually became a perennial. Annual grains need to be reseeded, while perennials regrow from their roots. That change is unheard of without complex hybridization.

In treated soil, microbial communities flourish, enabling the soil to oxidize hydrogen and actually manufacture water as a byproduct. That hydrosynthesis shows up in plant size, nutrition and resulting resilience against pests and harsh climates.

Water was turned off in a greenhouse using HumiSoil® in China during COVID-19. The workers returned to find it filled with huge, healthy melons with no added water. A trial in Aqaba, Jordan, demonstrated that additional moisture from Humisoil grass continued to be produced at incredibly high temperatures for a short period on the treated vs. untreated plots with no irrigation!

Chapter Six
GREENING ENERGY

Building Code Changes

Climate-conscious building codes are changing to require new construction to use more renewable building materials, increase energy efficiency with more insulation, well-sealed, dual-glazed windows, and solar-electric systems for all-electric power. Commercial buildings will be wired for EV charging. Some codes improve resilience against climate change impacts, such as flooding and tornadoes.

Mixed Energy Sources

Department of Energy's (DOE) Loan Programs Office (LPO), Jigar Shah says their modeling shows that the energy mix we need for the future includes: solar, wind, hydro, geothermal, biofuels, new nuclear, and green hydrogen.

U.S. Solar Electric Energy

The US Department of Energy forecasts that in 2025, solar will supply 93% of US electricity. Solar accounted for 56% of all new electricity-generating capacity added to the US grid in the first half of 2025. As of the end of 2024, the total installed capacity was over 100 GW, and it is expected to grow to about 174 GW by the end of 2025.

Wind Energy

Wind energy is currently the largest source of renewable electricity in the US, accounting for over 10% of the country's electricity generation and 154 GW of capacity. States like Iowa, South Dakota, and Kansas generate more than 40% of their electricity from wind.

New sites have slowed due to the phase-out of federal tax incentives. The industry has driven nearly $330 billion in investment over the last 20 years and supports over 300,000 jobs. The wind industry is increasingly replacing older turbines on existing sites with newer, more powerful ones, expanding capacity without building new wind farms.

Hydroelectric Energy

Most hydroelectric capacity is concentrated in the Pacific Northwest, providing about 6% of total electricity generation and 27% of renewable electricity. It relies on rainfall but has been a reliable and flexible energy source, accounting for 96% of utility-scale energy storage capacity through pumped-storage hydropower. Hydropower would benefit from upgrading existing facilities, adding capacity at non-powered dams, and adding battery storage to hydropower plants.

Geothermal Energy

The US is the world's leading geothermal energy producer with about 3.7 GW of installed capacity. New technology is finding expanded potential locations.

Closed-Loop Geothermal Systems circulate fluid through sealed underground pipes, eliminating the need for water injection into rock formations and making it less seismically risky.

Enhanced Geothermal Systems use long horizontal fractures and circulate fluid to harvest heat in impermeable rock.

Superhot Rock Geothermal wells of greater depths yield 5 to 10X more energy and can cost-compete with fossil fuels.

Old oil and gas wells are being repurposed for geothermal energy.

Federal and state incentives spur project development.

New Nuclear

New nuclear is greenish. Although a low-carbon source, it has significant environmental and safety challenges. But it produces virtually no greenhouse gases during operation, making it cleaner than fossil fuels. Concerns remain regarding the long-term storage of radioactive waste, the risk of accidents, and the environmental impact of uranium mining and plant construction. The new nuclear plants have passive rather than active safety systems, use modular rather than custom-built fixtures, but are still hard to build cost-effectively.

The new Georgia Votgle took 13 years and was the prototype for 6 more units, which they expect to build faster and more efficiently. Solar works about 25% of the time, wind about 50%, and nuclear 100%. Excess electrical energy can be converted to hydrogen for storage. Advanced fast reactors and molten salt reactors are both designed to use spent fuel from standard plants, significantly reducing the volume, toxicity, and lifespan of the waste.

ENERGY SECURITY

Using domestically produced biofuels from agricultural residues, dedicated energy crops like Paulownia and MegaFlora plantations, and waste streams enhances national energy security by reducing our reliance on imported petroleum. Decentralized rural cottage industries can process local organic waste into valuable products such as biofertilizers, biofuels, and new materials. Used within the community, this type of sustainable circular bioeconomy also creates jobs in rural communities.

DOE models consider macroeconomic factors like Gross Domestic Product (GDP) growth, income levels, and energy prices (e.g., crude oil, natural gas) and the availability and cost of resources, such as fossil fuels (oil, natural gas, coal), renewable energy sources (solar, wind, geothermal), and nuclear power. In 2023, a record 1.8 trillion was invested in clean energy, generating more revenue from environmentally friendly investing than from fossil fuel investments, and 6 million more people were employed in the clean energy sector than in 2019 global totals.

GROWING RENEWABLE FUELS

Biofuels: We can grow our own fuel. The DOE funds and makes loans for high-impact biotechnology research, development, and commercial-scale demonstration projects to lower the cost of advanced biofuels, as part of its strategy to advance clean energy and reduce emissions. The types of biofuel include: Ethanol and other Bioalcohols, Biodiesel, Green Diesel, Vegetable oil, Biogasoline, Bioethers & Sustainable Aviation Fuel (SAF). Biofuels are seen as critical for sectors where other options may not be available in the foreseeable future, such as SAF.

Biomass Gasification into Biochar

Biomass Gasification heats organic matter (biomass) using advanced technology described in chapter 9, which converts it into three categories:

- Solid Biochar
- Liquid Bio-Oil Fuel
- Syngas Fuel

The biomass first undergoes drying and pyrolysis, breaking it down into volatile gases and a solid black biochar, the carbon-rich material with many uses. The remaining volatile bio-oil and hydrogen-rich 'syngas' are cleaned of tar and other volatiles and further processed to convert them into a usable fuel. Syngas is generally composed of hydrogen (H2), carbon monoxide (CO), and trace amounts of methane (CH4), along with other components.

Renewable Diesel

Biochar production can convert the wood of fast-growing MegaFlora® into Renewable Diesel without any additional processing. Jet fuel can be 30% of the biodiesel. Renewable Diesel is a chemically similar replacement for petroleum-based diesel for current diesel engines.

Biofuels produced from wood and biomass waste can help reduce greenhouse gas emissions by 85% compared to petroleum-based diesel. Heavy metals and other inorganic contaminants often concentrate in biochar's solid residues. This material requires conscious management to prevent re-pollution. Since Biochar can be used as a soil amendment and managed with products containing humic substances, such as HumiSoil®, it can capture and bind heavy metals.

Alcohol Fuels: Ethanol has low energy yield, performance issues, corrosive effects on the engine and fuel systems if the fuel is left sitting. Ethanol's solvent properties can degrade rubber and plastic seals, gaskets, and fuel lines, potentially causing leaks in older cars.

Green Hydrogen

Green hydrogen is a clean energy source produced by splitting water into hydrogen and oxygen using electrolysis powered by renewable electricity from solar or wind power. This process is climate-neutral, emitting only water vapor, making it a promising fuel for decarbonizing sectors that are difficult to electrify directly, like steel production, shipping, and long-term energy storage.

Shah sees potential for hydrogen energy to decarbonize industrial sectors, such as steel and cement production, where emissions are difficult to reduce otherwise. He has been exploring loan guarantees to support a large-scale green hydrogen storage project in Utah.

This demonstrates that green hydrogen is a viable, necessary part of decarbonizing heavy industry because it is a clean-burning fuel for processes such as steel and chemical production, producing only zero-emission water vapor.

Hydrogen can replace coal in the steelmaking process to reduce iron ore, which is a significant source of emissions in the industry and is a crucial feedstock for producing ammonia and other chemicals, and is ideal for providing the high-temperature heat required in sectors like cement, glass, and aluminum manufacturing, where electrification is more challenging.

Hydrogen fuel is best used in fuel cells in vehicles such as long-haul trucks, buses, and construction equipment, where their high energy density, fast refueling times, and long range are critical. Hydrogen fuel cells are a better fit for these vehicles than batteries, which are often heavier and require longer charging times. We can grow our sustainable biofuels without depending on foreign imports!

Nikola Tesla & Electricity

Tesla invented the alternating current (AC) system, which is more efficient for transmitting electricity over long distances than Thomas Edison's direct current (DC). He also holds the patent for inventing the radio. Our current system of Wi-Fi, wireless charging, and cellular networks was inspired by Nikola Tesla's early concepts for wireless energy and communication.

Wi-Fi is a green option primarily because it enables more efficient use of renewable electricity than wired networks and offers significant potential for energy savings and environmental benefits. Wi-Fi reduces the need for extensive physical cabling, lowering energy consumption in some cases compared to wired infrastructure, and enables remote work and other digital services that decrease travel and physical resource use.

Chapter Seven
GREEN TRANSPORTATION

Energy-Conscious Options

Green transportation represents a fundamental shift towards a sustainable future. By embracing a combination of public transport, cycling, walking, electric vehicles, ride-sharing, and alternative fuels, individuals and policymakers can significantly reduce greenhouse gas emissions and improve air quality. As cities continue to develop and innovate, the transition to green transportation will be critical to creating healthier, more sustainable communities.

PUBLIC TRANSIT SYSTEMS

Public transit systems, including buses, trains, and subways, provide a viable alternative to individual car use, especially as they transition to biofuels or become electric vehicles. They are designed to move large numbers of people efficiently and can significantly reduce traffic congestion and greenhouse gas emissions.

Reduced Carbon Footprint: Public transit emits fewer pollutants per passenger mile compared to private vehicles. Trains and buses can carry many passengers at once, making them more energy-efficient.

Electric Buses: Many cities are transitioning to electric buses, which produce zero tailpipe emissions, further enhancing the sustainability of public transit.

High Speed Rail (HSR): This type of rail transportation system is crucial for addressing climate change by enabling sustainable transportation and reducing travel times and greenhouse gas emissions. Investing in HSR infrastructure also creates economic growth. Commuters get immediate benefits while the system builds environmental sustainability. Successful systems in countries like Japan, France, and China highlight how HSR can connect major urban centers, dramatically reducing travel times compared to conventional rail or road travel. HSR is a solution worth the investment for stakeholders worldwide.

BICYCLING

Cycling is one of the most environmentally friendly modes of transportation. Not only does it have a negligible carbon footprint, but it also promotes physical fitness and mental well-being. Bicycles do not produce emissions while in use.

Low infrastructure cost: Building bike paths and lanes costs significantly less compared to the maintenance of roads and highways.

Bike sharing programs: Many cities offer bike-sharing systems that allow residents and visitors to rent bikes for short trips, making cycling an accessible option.

E-Bicycles

Electric bikes (e-bikes) are bicycles equipped with a battery-powered motor that assists with pedaling. They blend traditional cycling with electric propulsion, offering riders an efficient and versatile mode of transportation that can significantly contribute to environmentally friendly urban mobility.

By reducing emissions, promoting energy efficiency, alleviating traffic congestion, and encouraging active lifestyles, e-bikes offer a viable solution to achieving cleaner, more sustainable transportation systems. As cities and individuals increasingly adopt e-bikes, they could play a crucial role in addressing urban transportation challenges and climate change.

Various Features: E-bikes typically include a battery, motor, and, sometimes, a controller. The motor provides varying levels of assistance, which can be adjusted based on rider preference and terrain. The different types of e-bikes include:

Pedelecs: Provide assistance only when the rider is pedaling,

Throttle-Controlled: Allow the rider to engage the motor with a throttle, similar to a scooter.

Speed Pedelecs: Capable of higher speeds and often require registration or a license in some regions.

Benefits:

Reduction in Greenhouse Gas Emissions: E-bikes produce significantly lower emissions than cars, particularly in urban environments. Their use can reduce reliance on fossil-fuel-powered vehicles, leading to decreased overall greenhouse gas emissions. E-bikes are generally more energy-efficient than traditional motor vehicles. They require less energy per mile traveled, making them a more sustainable option for short- to medium-distance commuting while reducing dependence on fossil fuels.

Reduced Traffic Congestion: E-bikes take up less road space and can navigate through traffic more easily than cars, contributing to reduced congestion in urban areas. Many trips taken by cars are short and could be covered by an e-bike, reducing the number of vehicles on the road.

Less Noise Pollution: Compared to motor vehicles, e-bikes are much quieter, contributing to reduced noise pollution in urban areas.

Sustainable Urban Development: The popularity of e-bikes can lead to the development of more bike lanes and supporting lower-cost infrastructure, fostering a culture of environment-tally friendly transportation.

ELECTRIC SCOOTERS & SKATEBOARDS

E-skateboards are similar to traditional skateboards but are equipped with electric motors that assist with propulsion. They are popular among young adults and commuters for their agility and ease of use. Electric scooters and skateboards are innovative, eco-friendly transportation options that help reduce greenhouse gas emissions, decrease traffic congestion, and promote sustainable urban mobility.

By leveraging their compact size and energy efficiency, these vehicles can help cities become more livable and less reliant on traditional fossil-fuel-based transportation, thus supporting broader environmental goals, as their popularity continues to grow. They could play a crucial role in reshaping urban transportation landscapes towards greater sustainability. Benefits:

Lightweight: E-scooters and e-skateboards are typically lightweight, equipped with a handlebar, a standing deck, and a battery-powered motor that assists with propulsion. They are often used for short-distance travel and are commonly available through shared mobility programs in cities.

Reduced Greenhouse Gas Emissions: E-scooters and e-skateboards powered by electricity produce zero tailpipe emissions, significantly reducing greenhouse gas emissions compared to traditional gasoline or diesel vehicles. When charged with renewable energy, the carbon footprint of e-scooter use is further reduced, making them an efficient option for urban commuting with quiet operation.

Decreased Traffic Congestion: E-scooters occupy less street space than cars and help reduce overall traffic congestion, leading to more efficient urban mobility and decreasing the number of vehicles on the road.

Support for Sustainable Urban Mobility Initiatives: E-scooters and e-skateboards are electric-powered and complement Public Transport. They can serve as a last-mile solution for connecting users to public transportation hubs.

WALKING

Walking is the simplest form of transportation and greatly minimizes environmental impact. It requires no external energy sources and produces no emissions. Benefits include fitness and community engagement in walkable neighborhoods; encourages social interaction and community building through wider sidewalks, pedestrian-only zones, and safe crosswalks.

ELECTRIC & HYBRID VEHICLES

The shift away from traditional internal combustion engine vehicles to electric (EVs) and hybrid vehicles is a monumental step toward reducing transportation-related emissions. Electric vehicles produce zero tailpipe emissions, while hybrids combine an internal combustion engine with electric power to enhance fuel efficiency. When charged with renewable energy sources, EVs can operate with minimal environmental impact.

CARPOOLING & RIDE-SHARE SERVICES

Services like Uber and Lyft, as well as specialized carpooling apps, help reduce the number of vehicles on the road, leading to decreased traffic congestion and emissions. Sharing rides can significantly reduce individual fuel costs. Fewer cars on the road lead to decreased wear and tear on road infrastructure and lower emissions. Car Services make car ownership less necessary. The reliable, on-demand nature of car services means urban residents can access transportation without the fixed costs of owning a car, such as insurance, maintenance, and parking. Research the best options in your area.

ELECTRIC PLANES

While not yet in widespread use for commercial passenger travel, many e-planes are already flying, used for things like flight training, cargo, and medical transport. Current battery technology doesn't yet match the energy density of jet fuel, limiting range and payload.

HYDROGEN VEHICLES

Vehicles powered by hydrogen fuel cell technology use a fuel cell stack to convert hydrogen gas into electricity, producing only water vapor as emissions. There are zero nitrous oxide emissions, but the weight (6,000 pounds) makes it very heavy, so they are being developed and tested for heavy-duty vehicles like long-haul trucks, buses, and construction equipment because they offer a long driving range, fast refueling times, and zero tailpipe emissions.

Cummins States that its hydrogen engines emit nearly zero carbon dioxide, and its fuel cell electric vehicles (FECVs) produce only water vapor. Cummins expects its 15-liter hydrogen internal combustion engine (H2-ICE) to enter full production in 2027.

The California Energy Commission (CEC) Clean Transportation Program plans for zero-emission vehicle infrastructure, including a hydrogen refueling network along major, heavily trafficked transportation routes, such as I-5 and CA-99 in the Central Valley. Construction of a statewide network of 200 stations is planned to be finished by 2027 to support a range of vehicles, aiming for self-sufficiency by 2030. Clean Cars 4 All offers grants to low-income people to scrap old cars for zero-emission vehicles (ZEVs), hybrids, or transit/e-bikes.

FUTURE TRANSPORTATION

Transit-Oriented Development urban planning promotes the development of residential, commercial, and recreational spaces near transit hubs, encouraging the use of public transportation. We can reduce travel needs by designing neighborhoods where essential services and workplaces are within walking distance. Creating inclusive transportation options ensures that all community members can participate.

Work-From-Home

The work-from-home option has been boosted recently by a beneficial ripple effect from COVID-19. People have returned to the workplace but have experienced that option.

Zoom Meetings

The use of Zoom virtual business meetings is estimated to have reduced travel by 47%, giving companies a 30% savings in business trip travel costs. Business trips for short meetings, called boomerang trips, have virtually disappeared. More necessary in-person trips with higher value have been prioritized as financial departments influence travel frequency. This further supports the use of virtual meetings, with annual travel cost savings averaging $11,000 per employee.

Self-Driving Vehicles - AVs

AVs our commercially operating in five cities at this writing. The environmental benefits are numerous, and AVs have the potential to contribute meaningfully to environmental sustainability and climate change mitigation.

Current status:

Reliability: Companies like Waymo, Tesla, and others have made significant headway in developing reliable autonomous systems. Tesla's current supervised Robo taxi is operating in Texas and San Francisco, California, and demonstrated the first fully autonomous consumer vehicle in June 2025. The car drove itself from the factory to the consumer's home, safely navigating city and highway environments without a human driver to prove the technology. It will take time and demonstration for the public to feel reassured about the reliability of this system. Technology does fail.

Capacity: Many AVs are capable of functioning in urban settings under certain conditions, but achieving full autonomy in all circumstances remains complex.

Testing standards: Establishing comprehensive safety and testing standards is crucial. The public and governmental bodies need assurance regarding the consistent safety and reliability of these vehicles.

Public concerns: Many consumers express concerns over safety, privacy, liability and job displacement.

Infrastructure investment: Private companies and the government's investment in smart roads, traffic management systems, etc., are also factors in building support.

Environmental benefits: Vehicle ride-sharing services could yield reduced traffic congestion, fewer accidents, improved fuel use, less need for parking spaces, and further decreased resource consumption. AVs can integrate into smart city frameworks, promoting sustainable development practices, optimized resource management, and reduced urban sprawl.

High Speed Rail

The viability of high-speed rail (HSR) is grounded in its ability to operate effectively in densely populated regions where demand for efficient transportation is high. Successful systems in countries like Japan, France, and China highlight how HSR can connect major urban centers, dramatically reducing travel times compared to conventional rail or road travel. Furthermore, technological advancements have significantly improved the safety, reliability, and operational efficiency of HSR, making it a competitive option compared to air travel and driving.

Chapter Eight
RESIDENTIAL ENERGY USE

Embracing energy-conscious options in residential settings benefits both the environment and homeowners seeking to reduce costs. By investing in energy-efficient products and smart technology and making behavioral changes, individuals can create sustainable living spaces that provide home comfort and mitigate climate change.

Small behavioral changes can yield significant energy savings:

Unplug Devices: Many electronics consume power even in standby mode, so unplug devices from power when they are not in use.

Adjust Your Thermostat: Set the thermostat a few degrees lower in winter and add warm layers before turning it up. Set the thermostats higher in summer and use ceiling fans or low noise electric fans where you are sitting or sleeping.

Maximize Laundry Efficiency: Run full loads of laundry in cold water whenever possible, using cold-water detergent. With gray water systems, use cold-water soaps formulated for septic tanks. Use your electric dryer only as much as you need to partially dry and de-wrinkle your clothes, and hang them in your bathroom to finish drying in arid climates, or use a clothesline in the sun.

SMART HOME ENERGY OPTIONS

Smart home devices facilitate greater control over energy use, and the technology is evolving. Homeowners can install smart equipment to optimize energy use.

Smart Thermostats: These devices learn your heating and cooling preferences and adjust temperatures only when necessary. They can reduce heating and cooling costs by up to 15%.

Smart Plugs: Allow you to control devices remotely and prevent them from drawing power when not in use.

Energy Monitors: Provide real-time energy consumption data, helping homeowners identify and reduce energy waste.

LED plug-ins: Lights that automatically turn on in the dark and off in light, that can be turned to angle up or down. Use for hallways and bathrooms.

Dirty electricity collector plug-ins: devices that plug into electrical outlets to reduce "dirty electricity," which are designed to enhance performance, reducing high-frequency disturbances or noise on a home's wiring, and increase longevity of electronics.

ENERGY-EFFICIENT APPLIANCES

Generally, choose ENERGY STAR® certified appliances. These appliances use less energy and water than standard models, providing significant savings.

Refrigerators: Energy-efficient refrigerators can use up to 50% less energy than older models.

DC/AC Refrigerators: There are several brands available now. We used Sun Frost refrigerators and freezers, which are outstandingly energy-efficient due to ergonomic design and unusually heavy insulation. They can be used in a home with solar power, an AC-to-DC converter, or other low-output energy sources.

All models are available in 12, 24, or 48-volt DC, as well as 110 and 220-volt AC. In a home using conventional utility power, energy consumption for refrigeration is typically cut by a factor of five!

Cooktop: Induction cooktops are 97% more efficient because they use electromagnetic energy to directly heat the cookware. They do require magnetic cookware, such as cast iron or stainless steel. They cook faster than gas, so there are no indoor pollutants from natural gas or propane. There is an automatic shut-off if the pot is removed. Their flat surface makes them easy to clean.

Air fryer: These ceramic-surfaced electric cookers that are are safe and more efficient than standard electric ovens for small to medium portions - like two chicken breasts. They use less power at lower temperatures and cook faster due to rapid air circulation.

Instant Pot: This updated electric pressure cooker is safer and more convenient than older stovetop models. It cooks countertop in a stainless steel pot with built-in heating and digital timers. It significantly cuts down the time for dishes like beans, whole grains, roasts, and stews, which typically take hours. Once a dish is started, it requires no stirring or babysitting.

Solar Box Oven: Various designs of solar box ovens have been used globally, in both sunny developing and developed nations, for economic, social, and environmental reasons. They reduce indoor air pollution while reducing fossil fuels. Buy a premade cooker or order plans for a DIY project. Cardboard boxes with aluminum foil will work, but they are the least permanent option.

Solar Dryer/Dehydrator: Buy one or find various DIY designs online. Our shallow solar dehydrator box with a plexiglass lid was used to dehydrate chopped vegetables for soup mix, make fruit leather, crackers, and granola. We also had 2' x 4' wooden frames with fiberglass screens to dry my herbs.

GoSun Solar Oven: This is designed for camping, but I use it in summer heat to keep my kitchen from making my air conditioner work harder. It uses a unique evacuated-glass-tube design with a 2-foot-long stainless-steel tray to hold the food, heated by highly reflective stainless-steel panels that fold like a clamshell for transport.

It uses only direct sunlight to cook, no matter the outside temperature. There are cautions to follow, but energy-free cooking is worth it. Ensure the oven is positioned correctly to maximize sunlight exposure and do not leave it unattended.

GoSun cooking times:

- Hot Dogs, pre-cooked: 15-30 Min.

• Fresh corn on the cob: 20-30 Min.

• Quinoa or Brown Rice 50-75 Min.

• Root vegetable chunks: 30-90 Min.

• Biscuits, or Quick Breads 20-30 Min.

• Raw Chicken cutlets or tenders: 60-90 Min.

• Beans soaked overnight: 2-3 Hours

Solar clothes dryer: UV rays from the sun are a natural sanitizer, and outdoor clothesline drying provides a fresh, clean scent.

Washing Machines: Front-loading household washers typically consume less water and energy. There are manual and portable washing machine options for use in tiny spaces and for travel.

Dishwashers: Modern dishwashers are designed to use less water and energy, especially when run on eco-friendly settings. Manual dishwashing with a continuous stream of water is equivalent to a full dishwasher cycle, but washing a few dishes makes handwashing more efficient.

ENERGY EFFICIENT DESIGN & FIXTURES

Natural Lighting: Maximizing natural light by utilizing energy-efficient windows and skylights. Reflective surfaces can also reduce the need for artificial lighting.

Energy-efficient Windows & French doors: The best replacement windows typically feature double- or triple-pane glass for superior insulation, low-e coatings to reduce energy loss, and durable frames made from materials such as vinyl, fiberglass, or wood. Additionally, the best home windows come with strong warranties and high energy-efficiency ratings, ideal for long-term performance and savings.

Window protection: Thermal-insulating +/or 100% sun-blocking drapes can be used alone or combined with a variety of light- and temperature-controlling window treatments, such as standard or smart window shades, honeycomb cellular shades, motorized blinds and shades, & shutters. Curtains can also protect furniture from sun damage and also absorb and dampen sound.

Skylights & Solatube: This is a tube design with different feature options that brings in superior, leak-proof natural light with easier installation than standard skylights. They require no changes in your roof framing. Different diffusers can be used to dim or control how light enters the room. Add-on kits can provide additional electric lighting after dark. They help reduce air conditioning load by dispersing heat above the ceiling insulation, which also puts less strain on your HVAC unit.

Energy-Efficient Lighting: LEDs use up to 75% less energy than incandescent bulbs and last much longer. LED lighting is one of the most effective ways to reduce lighting energy consumption.

Water purification: Now there are highly efficient countertop, under-sink and travel systems discussed in Chapter 5.

INSULATION & SEALING

Proper building insulation and sealing can significantly reduce energy use:

Renewable cellulose insulation made from recycled paper is denser and has a higher R-value than fiberglass insulation. Manufacture and installation emit fewer GHGs to achieve the same insulating performance as glass, mineral, or plastic insulation in new and retrofit buildings.

Fiberglass can irritate the skin, eyes, and respiratory passages from inhaling fibers or from contact, causing itching, redness, coughing, and wheezing.

Reflectix: Aluminum-covered bubble wrap; this is considered a green product due to its energy-saving, non-toxic, fiber-free composition. It is easy to handle and flexible. It can also wrap a hot water heater.

Sealing: Sealing gaps around doors and windows can prevent drafts and increase the overall efficiency of your heating and cooling systems. Fabric tubes filled with sand can be used as additional insulation on windowsills. Use a combination of materials, such as caulk for gaps around windows and weatherstripping for moving parts. Use painter's caulk or rope caulk for small gaps. For large gaps, use non-expanding foam sealant. For moving parts, use adhesive-backed weatherstripping, and add a door sweep to the bottom of exterior doors.

SOLAR SOLUTIONS

Solar energy systems allow homeowners to harness renewable energy and significantly decrease reliance on the grid. Passive solar design includes building orientation, strategic window placement, roof overhang and thermal mass to heat and cool spaces naturally.

Solar Panels: Expensive Photovoltaic (PV) panels generate electricity and may qualify for tax reductions or rebates. But there are other solar-assisted solutions for homes:

Solar Water Heaters: These systems use solar energy to heat water for domestic use. We made a passive box solar water heater shown in Chapter 3.

Solar Water Heaters purchase: For cold climates, consider units with evacuated-tube designs, which retain heat better on cloudy days. Active systems use a pump to circulate the water. Back-up heating is always a necessity.

Solar Space Heaters: Use an attached greenhouse or solar box collectors that can vent heat into the structure, controlled by removing or insulating hatches.

HEATING SYSTEMS

Energy-efficient heating and cooling systems can yield substantial savings:

High-Efficiency Furnaces: Look for systems with Annual Fuel Utilization Efficiency (AFUE) ratings for furnaces.

Heat Pumps: These systems are highly efficient, transferring heat rather than generating it, leading to significant reductions in energy use.

High-Efficiency Air Conditioners: Look for systems with high Seasonal Energy Efficiency Ratio (SEER) ratings for air conditioners.

Standard Radiant Floors are efficient at reducing energy costs because they heat from the ground up, and heat rises naturally. This provides even warmth compared to forced air systems, but the upfront cost can be high. It uses a network of water-filled pipes is embedded in slab concrete with insulation below it or below tile floors, and requires a water heater.

Biochar Concrete Radiant Floors: Adding biochar to concrete makes the concrete stronger and reduces its carbon footprint by 40%. Running electrical wires through the slab mixed with conductive types of biochar allows the concrete to be heated when an electrical current is active. This energy-efficient radiant heating system is faster to install and more efficient to operate. It warms the entire floor evenly, reducing energy loss from ductwork and operating at a lower temperature than forced-air systems. Industrial graphene is another emerging option.

NATURAL COOLING SYSTEMS

Screen doors: Use standard metal or simple fabric screen doors in secure areas. to allow cool night air to circulate. This is more efficient when combined with cross-ventilation from open windows. Durable, inexpensive, and easy to install, fiber screen doors split in the middle and attach with Velcro strips around the sides and top.

Fans: From ancient handheld fans to tabletop or freestanding electric fans, these are an efficient option for spot or area cooling. Look for quiet operation and easy cleaning.

WATER CONSERVATION SYSTEMS

Low-Flow Fixtures: Faucets and shower heads. These energy-efficient fixtures use technologies like aerators to reduce water use by 20%-40% while maintaining performance.

Low-flush toilets: Newer low-flush toilets are up to 60% more efficient and provide a powerful flush with less water. They are gravity-fed, pressure-assisted, or dual flush. Dual flush may offer a low flow of 1.28 gallons per flush (gpf) and a higher flow of the federal standard 1.6 gpf.

Waterless toilets are designed for off-grid cabins and cost from $200 to $2000, offering superior performance.

Waterless urinals: Currently cost $100 to $600 and use a cartridge with a liquid sealant to trap odor-causing gases while allowing urine to drain into the plumbing system. Cartridges cost $10-15 and need to be replaced once or twice a year, depending on use level.

Conservation: Limiting showers to three minutes helps. In Mexico, I used a shower with a rooftop cistern that caught rainwater above the shower stall.

Heat Pump Water Heaters: These are significantly more efficient than traditional electric water heaters.

Tankless Water Heaters: Natural gas or propane tankless heaters are faster and produce endless water, but may be more expensive to operate. Electric units cost less but have slower flow rates and may limit simultaneous use. Innovations discussed later are making this option more efficient.

Electric hot water pot: Heat water with electric power and store the unused portion in a thermos to retain heat.

Rainwater Collection: A storage tank (cistern) is required for rainwater collection. There are now roof gutters that will filter out leaves for lower maintenance:

Polyethylene (Poly) plastic tanks, NSF 61 certified for drinking water, are versatile and economical. They come in various sizes and can be installed above or below ground; they resist rust and corrosion.

Galvanized steel tanks: Made of zinc-coated polymer-lined steel to prevent zinc from leaching into the potable water, these are strong, durable and recyclable.

Fiberglass tanks: Lightweight, durable, rust and chemical-resistant and can withstand UV rays, and do not leach substances.

Concrete: Durable, natural insulating properties and 80-year life. A natural antibacterial material that prevents bacterial and algal growth, but has a significant carbon footprint from transportation and cement emissions. Emissions can be reduced 40% when combined with biochar.

Slimline tanks: For properties with limited space, slimline tanks offer more storage than a rain barrel but are narrow enough to fit against walls or in tight areas.

INDOOR AIR FILTRATION

HEPA indoor air filters have special filters that trap 99.97% of microscopic allergens from airborne particles such as dust, pollen, mold, and smoke that are 0.3 micrometers or larger. Models with carbon filters also remove odors and gases.

Air Doctor: Uses a multi-stage filtration system, including an UltraHEPA filter that captures 99.99% of particles as small as 0.003 microns in size. It also has a carbon filter to remove gases, odors, and VOCs, which a standard HEPA filter does not address.

Whole-house fans: These are found to improve indoor air quality by constantly pulling fresh outdoor air through windows and exhausting polluting indoor air and moisture out through the attic, removing allergens and odors.

SUSTAINABLE LANDSCAPING

Landscaping can also contribute to energy consumption reduction while feeding on CO2. Check with your power company to see a list of approved trees to avoid problems with power lines.

Native Plants: These require less water and maintenance, which can reduce energy used for irrigation. Check the web for natives for your climate zone.

Drought-tolerant plants: Look for non-native, drought-tolerant plants like Mediterranean herbs that are ornamental and have culinary uses.

Xeriscape: This type of landscaping is designed to reduce water and pesticide use as well as maintenance. With periodic droughts, California has encouraged people to replace lawns in favor of drought-tolerant plants that also provide habitat for local wildlife. Xeriscapes can reduce water bills by 75% compared to traditional landscaping.

Shade Arbors: Edible landscaping design includes building an arbor over a south or west-facing door and/or windows, which can support deciduous vines and climbing food plants in hot weather but lose their foliage in winter. This creates a passive cooling effect on the house in hot weather that naturally disappears in the cold seasons for passive solar heat gain.

Permaculture Design: There are many websites discussing permaculture solutions for landscaping and gardening. The system encourages people to plant culinary herbs and other food plants near the kitchen door for easy access. It favors perennial plants over annuals and different plant heights for multiple uses in your biodiverse landscape design.

Chapter Nine
GREEN CONSTRUCTION & INDUSTRY

Important climate-friendly goals for industry include: increased use of renewables; carbon capture and storage; advanced waste management, including recycling and waste-to-energy systems; water purification; and energy-efficient transportation that focuses on reducing GHG emissions, conserving natural resources, and reducing pollution.

Recycled & Reclaimed Materials:

Deconstructing buildings can preserve building materials and the embodied energy they contain, including steel, glass, and wood. Steel and glass are durable and can be recycled repeatedly without losing strength, significantly reducing the need for raw materials and the energy required to extract them. Lumber that can't be reused can be composted or made into biochar.

REGENERATIVE MATERIALS

Bamboo: A fast-growing, strong, and renewable grass that absorbs more CO2 than trees, regrows from roots after harvest. Overharvesting is a problem in Southwest China, Japan, India, and parts of South America due to high demand for edible bamboo shoots, paper, and timber, which are turning natural Forests into monocultures that are harmful to native species and the soil.

Hempcrete: A bio-composite made from hemp hurds, lime, and water, which is carbon-negative and an excellent insulator.

Biochar: A charcoal-like substance made from wood or biomass waste from farms, forests and landfills, with multiple uses for manufacturing and construction. Producing biochar sequesters carbon and creates liquid and gas fuels as byproducts. Used as a soil amendment and to improve animal health and reduce manure odors. Also used in water and air filtration, in products like plastics, paints, health and cosmetic products, and renewable graphene.

Concrete & Biochar or Renewable Graphene: The mixture reduces concrete's carbon footprint by 40% with biochar and 50% with renewable graphene, while becoming more durable with enhanced thermal properties.

Industrial Renewable Graphene: a multi-use sustainable choice.

Fly ash & Concrete: Fly ash is a byproduct of coal combustion in power plants. Replace a portion of cement in concrete with fly ash to reduce the carbon footprint.

Laminated Timber: Glulam beams and columns are wooden beams or panels made from layers of lumber bonded with adhesives. They are a more sustainable option than concrete and steel and are appropriate in some applications.

Cork: Cork from the cork oak tree soil crate is highly regulated for sustainable harvesting.

Soils: Adobe brick is an ancient, sustainable clay building material. Increasing focus on green building and low-carbon materials is boosting interest in **Rammed Earth & Soilcrete** as sustainable alternatives that offer excellent thermal mass and low-emissions construction, used to create foundations, control erosion, and form low-cost roads and pathways.

INNOVATIVE BUILDING METHODS

3D printing: allows the creation of structures with minimal waste. Some innovations even use materials like soil and seeds that can grow and strengthen the building over time.

Green Roofs: These are a hallmark of sustainable construction. They act as an insulating layer to regulate temperature, absorb stormwater, improve air quality, and provide habitats for wildlife.

Rainwater Harvesting: capturing roof rainwater for irrigation and toilet flushing.

Water Reuse: Treating and reusing on-site water reduces the need to transport large volumes of water.

CarbonCure Technology: Involves injecting captured CO_2 into concrete during mixing, turning it into calcium carbonate mineralization to reduce emissions and improve its strength.

Biochar in Concrete & Asphalt: Companies are using carbon-negative biochar from local waste streams, which stores carbon long-term within the built environment, creating a circular bioeconomy, reducing the carbon footprint, and preventing methane emissions from typical landfill disposal.

COOLING EFFICIENCY

The most interesting emerging technologies for cooling spaces improve energy efficiency by integrating smart controls and eliminating harmful refrigerants. Solid-state cooling is an eco-friendly, refrigerant-free alternative to traditional air conditioning by manipulating material properties to absorb or release heat, with technologies like thermoelectric cooling and caloric cooling leading the way for compact, quiet, efficient cooling in devices from laptops to refrigerators.

Solid-State Cooling is a revolutionary class of technology that uses magnetocaloric, elastocaloric, and thermoelectric materials that heat up or cool down in response to applied magnetic fields, pressure, or voltage changes. These systems have few or no moving parts, enabling silent operation, reduced maintenance, and the elimination of traditional, high global-warming-potential (GWP) refrigerants.

Recent breakthroughs in nano-engineered thermoelectric films, increasingly made from graphene, have doubled the efficiency of some devices at room temperature. The most energy-efficient buildings often incorporate features like cube or dome shapes, which minimize heat loss, use sustainable materials, and are designed to generate their own renewable energy.

ENERGY EFFICIENT BUILDINGS

The most energy-efficient LEED-certified buildings often incorporate features such as cube or dome shapes, which minimize heat loss; use sustainable materials; and are designed to generate their own renewable energy through AI-controlled air conditioning, ground-source heat pumps, and advanced process controls to minimize energy consumption.

Key Features:

Insulation: Invest in high-performance insulation for walls, the attic, and the roof.

Materials: Prioritize sustainable and recycled materials.

Energy-efficient Doors, Windows & Lighting: high-performance energy-saving windows and French doors that provide natural light, LED light fixtures, Solatube skylights with LED lighting, and energy-efficient appliances.

On-site renewable energy: Solar panels or other renewable energy sources directly into the building design.

GREEN BUILDING TYPES:

Tiny House movement: the rise of tiny houses reduces all the materials required for current residential construction.

Adobe Buildings: Owner-builder projects can use this ancient, sustainable system with high thermal mass for energy efficiency.

Greater World Earthships: the community near Taos, New Mexico, is home to over 100 of these off-the-grid homes. These structures continue to be a sustainable model for living, using solar and wind power and recycled materials to provide shelter, energy, and a self-sufficient lifestyle.

Earth-bermed House: The temperature of the Earth moderates at 12 to 40 feet below the surface. An earth-sheltered home is built into a hillside to cover and insulate one or more walls, or the roof as well. An exposed front allows for natural light and passive solar heating. An existing mobile home or trailer can be bermed into a hillside, with appropriate drainage.

This provides passive moderation of variations in outside temperatures. The benefits may be worth the cost of dealing with local and state building codes and zoning regulations, which may affect the buildable area. Site development is complex and requires structural engineering.

Underground building: Fresno, CA, has a unique underground home. It was hand-dug from hardpan soil and built by Baldasare Forestiere from 1906 until his death in 1946. He created an underground home with a summer bedroom and a winter bedroom, a bath, a functional kitchen, a fish pond, a parlor with a fireplace, archways, grottoes, and courtyards. Sky holes bring in natural light above his fruit trees and allow his underground garden to flourish today.

Energy-efficient prefab homes: Built with sealed connections to minimize air leakage and with all the energy conservation features previously listed, can save homeowners on energy bills. Factory-built units offer better quality control, reduced waste, and shorter construction time, resulting in lower costs compared to traditional housing.

GREEN BIOMINING TECHNOLOGY

Biomining uses microorganisms to extract metals from ores and waste materials. Techniques like bioleaching, which use bacteria and an acidic solution to dissolve metals, make it an environmentally friendly alternative to traditional mining methods. Ores and waste materials are prepared for microbial treatment, which can involve crushing the ore. Then microorganisms, typically bacteria like *Thiobacillus ferrooxidans* or fungi, are introduced to the material.

The microbes metabolize the metals, producing acids or other compounds that break down the minerals, releasing the metals into a liquid solution. That metal-rich solution is separated from the solid material. Then the metal is recovered from the solution. Biomining primarily targets metals such as copper, gold, nickel, cobalt, zinc, and uranium, but is also being explored for rare earth elements.

RECYCLABLE BIOPLASTIC

Bioplastics are made from renewable plant-based materials like corn, sugarcane, potatoes, or algae. Recent development of a recyclable bioplastic derived from high-cellulose biomass, such as straw, utilizes steam explosion technology, which exposes the biomass to high-temperature steam.

The steam bursts the plant cells apart, optimizing digestion in a microbial fermentation process used to release glucose. This glucose is then metabolized by specific microbes, producing lipids that serve as the raw material for bioplastic production. The bioplastic can be recycled multiple times and even regenerated through microbial reprocessing.

The company has ingeniously combined its bioplastic liner with a recyclable paper exterior, with an air gap in between. This unique construction allows users to safely hold the cup filled with hot beverages, while the insulating airspace keeps the outside warm without becoming too hot. Using this cup, coffee shops can eliminate the need for additional paper sleeves to protect customers' hands.

After use, a tab is pulled to easily separate the bioplastic from the paper. The bioplastic goes in one recycling bin, while the paper goes into another. Reducing environmental waste this way could also contribute to a circular bioeconomy for a more sustainable future.

Current plastic container manufacturing has problems. Despite good intentions, the State of California has had difficulties effectively recycling biodegradable or compostable plastics.

Industrial composters are mandated to accept compostable plastics; however, they lack reliable methods to sort them from traditional plastics. Additionally, consumers can also find recycling guidelines confusing, or just don't care, leading to contaminated waste streams.

If plastics were universally recyclable by requiring the widespread implementation of bioplastic technologies, we would be more likely to effectively divert them from landfills. South Korea has the most recycling options, with specific bins for: food, vinyl, PET, styrofoam, glass, and metals, plus laws banning hard-to-recycle PVC and colored plastics.

RENEWABLE GREEN GRAPHENE

Graphene is the thinnest, strongest material known. It is a thin, flexible engineered carbon material with a one-atom-thick layer of carbon atoms arranged in a hexagonal lattice, known for its ability to efficiently absorb and conduct heat and electricity. Renewable green graphene can interact with a wide range of electromagnetic wavelengths and has numerous exciting uses. Safety issues related to potential lung damage from inhalation are being studied.

The cost of graphene production can vary widely depending on the quality and production method. Expensive chemical-reduction production drove the market price to an average of $100 US per gram for very high-purity graphene. It was produced in small quantities using reducing agents, which are dangerous to people and the environment. That has slowed its potential uses.

Renewable graphene is biologically sourced, so prices depend on type, quality, and application. Higher-purity, research-grade materials can cost $500 per gram, but industrial-grade materials can cost less than $1 per gram. The more affordable cost of renewable graphene is transforming emerging technologies. High-quality, renewable green graphene is produced using two methods that do not rely on hazardous reducing agents, making it cheaper and more environmentally safe to produce.

Concentrating Solar Power (CSP) passive technology uses mirrors to concentrate sunlight to provide the even, high temperatures needed to decompose wood (pyrolysis) into biochar to make graphene using renewable energy and waste materials. Currently, industrial-grade graphene powders can range from around $25 to $75 per pound.

The second process is Flash Joule Heating. It can produce graphene in seconds using a high-voltage electrical pulse, making it more efficient for high-volume, scalable production. The cost is about $0.25 per pound.

TECHNOLOGIES

Hot water: Graphene-based heating panels used to replace hot water heater elements or for on-demand at each faucet. It can be used to improve the efficiency of heat pipes.

Heating systems: Highly efficient, lightweight, and flexible heating systems, such as those for underfloor heating, car seats, and windshield anti-fogging equipment. As paint, it can be heated quickly and uniformly with minimal energy waste.

Cooling electronics: can recharge faster and dissipate heat from electronic devices more efficiently, improving the cooling properties of graphene film.

Cooling electronics: Graphene's properties allow for both passive cooling (heat spreading) and active cooling (thermoelectric effect), and its low density makes it ideal for lightweight, thin electronic cooling solutions.

Packaging: Graphene oxide coating protects containers with more durable, biodegradable properties, replacing harmful PFAS.

Footwear: It strengthens the rubber outsoles and enhances the energy return of the foam midsoles.

Flexible touch sensors: Make high-performance, durable, and transparent touchscreens and wearable sensors that are resistant to stretching and bending.

Bendable screens: Their transparency, flexibility, and high electrical conductivity enable lighter, more durable electronic devices.

Wearable technology: Textiles infused with graphene offer heating, energy storage, and sensing capabilities while remaining flexible and are useful for durable smart fabrics for health monitors.

Road construction: It can make asphalt, concrete and paint more durable while lowering CO2 emissions.

Automotive/Aerospace industries: it makes lighter and stronger composite materials, enhanced batteries and super capacitors, conductive coatings for EMI/ESD shielding and corrosion protection, and is useful for aerospace de-icing systems.

Lightbulb: It made the thinnest light bulb in the world.

Water filter: Cutting-edge one-atom-thick graphene oxide membranes can be used for water purification and desalination systems. It blocks contaminants like salts, bacteria, viruses, and other impurities while allowing clean water or gas to pass through at a high flow rate.

Batteries: Makes higher-capacity, faster-charging lithium-ion batteries and super capacitors for electric vehicles and renewable energy storage. Faster charging (minutes) and a longer lifespan (thousands of cycles).

Passive radiant heat: Renewable graphene film or paint used on or integrated into pre-cast concrete panel flooring creates radiant heated floors with no maintenance for the 30+ year lifespan of the concrete! One company has introduced a panelized graphene radiant heat system. Requires a small amount of electricity from wires embedded in the concrete.

Renewable Graphene can also be produced using a portion of the biomass to generate heat during the gasification process. That process can use MegaFlora and other cellulosic, woody biomass of plant cell walls as feedstocks, converting them into liquid and gas biofuels in addition to biochar. Production innovations focus on scaling up production to reduce costs while maintaining material quality.

Radiant Heat: The thermal conductivity of renewable graphene infused concrete flooring with integrated electrical elements creates radiant heated floors for uniform warmth with no maintenance for the lifespan of the concrete. They use more electricity but heat up faster, are simpler to install, and have no boiler or water-pipe leakage, unlike circulating water (hydronic) systems. Energy-efficient heat pumps or solar hot water can reduce hydronic system costs.

RENEWABLE GRAPHENE BATTERIES

Graphene Batteries: Incorporate graphene into batteries to increase speed, efficiency, and capacity. *Example:* Samsung SDI has developed a "graphene ball" material that can increase battery capacity by 45% and charge 5Xs faster than standard lithium-ion batteries.

Batteries: Emerging technology using renewable green graphene can provide high-capacity energy storage by using copper covered with protective graphene that interacts with magnesium, without the need for lithium, cobalt, or other rare-earth mining. The magnesium converts to magnesium oxide, found in antacid digestive formulas. Used batteries could be regenerated by adding highly available, low-cost, magnesium.

Graphene-based batteries can be half the weight of standard of standard lithium-ion batteries, and more durable with a projected 25-year lifespan or more, while providing 2 Xs the capacity.

Thermal runaway, a well-known problem with lithium-ion batteries, has been shown not to be an issue with graphene batteries. Graphene-enhanced batteries could offer up to three times the energy density of current lithium-ion batteries in a smaller, lighter package.

SALT BATTERIES

Excess salt generated from the desalination of seawater, often referred to as brine, presents both challenges and opportunities. While its disposal can be environmentally concerning due to its high salinity, there is emerging interest in potential using it in battery technology.

The excess salt generated from desalinating seawater presents an opportunity, particularly in developing sodium-ion batteries and enhancing electrolyte solutions. However, significant research, development, and testing are needed to ensure economic viability and performance efficacy. Renewable graphene film may help.

Sodium-Ion Batteries are one of the most direct applications for the salt from desalination plants which could reduce production costs.

Brine as an Electrolyte: The high ionic concentration of brine can be investigated as a potential electrolyte in various battery systems. This may enhance conductivity and potentially lead to higher energy density. Researchers are exploring the use of brine components to create ionic liquids, which may yield improved performance characteristics for batteries at lower cost..

Battery Temperature Management: Salt solutions can have favorable thermal properties, which could be useful in managing the heat generated during battery operations. Effective heat management is critical in extending battery life and efficiency.

Sustainable Practices: Incorporating waste streams from desalination into battery technologies can lead to more sustainable production practices, once remaining challenges are addressed.

SMART CITIES

19 Smart Cities Now: Leading smart cities include Zürich, Oslo, Copenhagen and London. based on criteria like technology, infrastructure, and quality of life. Other cities frequently mentioned as smart are Amsterdam, Helsinki, Tokyo, and Seoul, which are known for their use of technology in areas such as public services, traffic management, and sustainability.

Barcelona, Spain: has deployed a municipal network of optical fiber, free public Wi-Fi, and sensors to monitor air quality and other environmental factors.

Singapore: has implemented a "Smart Nation" initiative that includes contactless public transport payments, digital health systems. They plan for a new vehicle-free eco-city in Tengah with a car-free town center with underground roads for vehicles, a 100-meter-wide forest corridor, community farming areas, and an energy-efficient centralized cooling system.

Smart cities of the future can use technology and data networks to improve the quality of life for citizens by creating efficient, sustainable, and responsive urban environments. Key features include interconnected infrastructure for smart transportation and energy, integrated communication networks like 5G, and the use of AI to optimize city services, public safety, and citizen engagement.

Examples:

Integrated Technology: They will have a vast, integrated network of sensors, devices, and computer systems that collect and analyze data to manage urban systems.

Advanced Infrastructure: This includes high-speed internet, smart energy grids, intelligent traffic management, and advanced waste management systems.

Sustainability: They will focus on reducing environmental impact through energy-saving buildings, smart waste disposal, efficient public transport, and the use of renewable energy.

Citizen-Centric Services: Technology will be used to improve daily life through applications like telemedicine, smart homes, and personalized education platforms.

Smart Mobility: This will involve a focus on sustainable options like public transport, cycling, and autonomous vehicles, with systems designed to optimize traffic flow.

Enhanced Governance and Security: Digital tools will increase citizen engagement in governance, while data analysis will strengthen security and resilience.

Data-Driven Decision Making: Large datasets from sensors and other sources will be analyzed using AI to help city leaders make more informed decisions.

SMART TECHNOLOGY ISSUES

The problems that have shown up related to Smart Technology that affect individual users in smart homes have broader implications in smart cities and industrial settings that need to be addressed:

Security: There is a lack of built-in authentication security features which creates vulnerability to cyber attacks. Concerns exist about third-party access to sensitive personal data collected from voice assistants and security cameras. Hackers could potentially gain control of smart locks, security systems, or even industrial control systems, leading to physical security breaches or operational disruptions that threaten safety.

Technical Reliability: Technology fails and troubleshooting smart devices can be complex for non-tech savvy users. Smart devices rely heavily on a stable Internet connection which makes them vulnerable to overcrowded network or power outage causing malfunction. Lack of universal standards causes user frustration from incompatibility for devices from different manufacturers.

Multiple Apps: This leads to multiple apps to control different devices. Rapid technological upgrades can make devices become prematurely obsolete due to manufacturers ending support services, or battery-powered devices draining quickly.

Social & Ethical Problems: the high cost of Smart Tech and the need for reliable internet access can exclude low-income and elderly populations. This can exacerbate existing social and economic inequalities, as access to essential services increasingly moves online.

Excessive reliance on smart technology for everyday tasks like navigation or memory can potentially weaken human math and problem-solving skills. Concerns about surveillance, data misuse, and automation can lead to public apprehension or resistance to smart city initiatives. Building public trust requires transparent communication and a focus on responsible use and robust regulation.

A significant concern about AI combined with Robotics is the potential for automation replacing numerous jobs, leading to increased unemployment and income inequality. Ethical considerations surrounding autonomous decision-making by AI and potential for misuse in areas like law enforcement and healthcare, where biased algorithms can perpetuate systemic inequalities, plus the existential risks from unlimited development of superintelligence.

Consideration should be given to the environmental impact of deploying advanced robotics, including vast energy consumption and waste generation that pose sustainability challenges. In order to harness the benefits of AI and robotics while mitigating these issues, stakeholders must limit development of thinking AI, limiting functions to rapid information gathering. We need to prioritize policies that promote responsible innovation, workforce retraining, and inclusive urban development.

Chapter Ten
HEALTHCARE

Virtual Medical Care: Virtual Telehealth meetings for doctors improve access to care without travel. Benefits include helping to address physician shortages, increased patient satisfaction, and easier continuous chronic disease management. It is especially beneficial for seniors and people too ill to drive. Being able to contact a doctor virtually for an emergency consult is a great advantage. Limitations include the inability to perform physical exams and potential disparities in access for those without the required technology. Research is required on the long-term effects of using the system.

Health Monitoring Clothing: Hexoskin is a type of smart clothing made of fabric with sensors that monitor heart rate, breathing, and motion.

Smart Fabric Monitors: Emerging technologies are developing more accurate and comfortable options with the potential to also diagnose disease more precisely, enabling detailed diagnostics for use in scientific research and professional sports.

Dr Zach Bush: MEDICINAL FOOD

Dr. Zach Bush, a physician, scientist, and educator focused on the connection between diet, the microbiome, human health, and the environment. He is triple board-certified in Internal Medicine, Endocrinology, and Hospice/Palliative Care. His non-profit, The Farmers Footprint, supports regenerative agriculture as a root-cause solution for both human and ecological health.

He researched the human microbiome and the damaging effects of glyphosate, the active ingredient in the herbicide Roundup, the first biocide to penetrate the human cell and cross the blood-brain barrier. A significant part of his work focused on the damaging effects of glyphosate and other toxins on the body's natural defense systems, and how to counteract them.

Depending on age, diet, and overall health, the human gut contains around 1,000 different species of beneficial bacteria, totaling 100 trillion. Glyphosate killing these beneficial bacteria, viruses & fungi prevents our body from making glutathione, which supports detox and activates our anti-inflammatory reactions.

Body Intelligence causes our cells to undergo a daily self-diagnostic process, and those that are damaged are naturally programmed to self-destruct (apoptosis). Our digestive system and lungs are the first line of defense against pathogens and defend the body from invasion.

Cell construction and renovation are going on when we ingest and digest food during the day, and maintenance garbage crews come at night to remove the waste. That amazing system relies on beneficial bacteria, viruses, and fungi, collectively called the microbiome, and the cleanest microbiome fuel is organic whole foods.

Glyphosate-based herbicides are toxic and act as an "endocrine disruptor" in the human body, which can cause microbiome damage, disrupt cellular communication pathways, leading to immune system dysfunction, and various diseases.

DNA HEALTHCARE

We all have unique DNA. That genetic profile shapes who we are and the health issues we struggle with. We can't change our genes, but Dr. J Dunn developed the diagnostic DNA-related system that gives patients targeted nutritional supplements to support their methylation - how the body turns off the damaging genes and turns on those that support optimal physical, mental and emotional health. Clean food becomes our most important self-healing option.

Methylation is critical for maintaining optimal health and plays a crucial role in several vital physiological processes, including:

- Energy Production: conversion of nutrients into usable energy.
- Nutrient Conversion: bioavailability and use.
- Fat Metabolism: aids breakdown and use.
- Hormone Production and Regulation: for hormonal balance.
- Immune Response: response to pathogens.
- Cholesterol Level Regulation: healthy cholesterol levels.
- Cardiovascular Risk Reduction: protective role.
- Detoxification Processes: elimination of toxins.

- Neurotransmitter Synthesis: regulating mood and cognition.
- Environmental and Emotional Stress Responses: modulation.
- Cancer Prevention: by reducing potential gene expression.

Dr. Dunn's practitioners evaluate individual methylation patterns through her extensive genetic (DNA) testing once, eliminating the need for repeated, expensive tests. Practitioners use muscle testing (Applied Kinesiology) at every appointment to rapidly determine the individualized dose and frequency of targeted pharmaceutical-grade nutritional supplements needed at that point in time to increase the individual's methylation capacity.

See: *Wholistic Methylation online: https://wholisticmethylation.com/methylation/ and YouTube: Dr. J Dunn videos.*

WELLNESS SYSTEMS

There are many systems based on different philosophies and technologiesthat may use a combination of practices to promote wellness and prevent illness: Nutritional Supplements, Aromatherapy, Massage systems, Meditation, Osteopathy, Reiki, Self-Healing Movement, Tai Chi, Western Herbology & Yoga, Bach Flower Remedies, Far Infrared Ray, Hyperbaric Oxygen Therapy, Pulsed Electromagnetic Frequency Therapy (PEMF), Healing Clay, and Healing Music.

ALTERNATIVE MEDICAL SYSTEMS

Ayurveda: This ancient Indian system uses a variety of approaches, including diet, herbs, massage, and yoga, to balance the mind, body, and spirit, based on the patient's body type: *Pitta (fire), Vata (air), or Kapha (water).*

Traditional Chinese Medicine (TCM): This agent holistic system is based on the belief in a vital life force called "qi" (Chi) that flows through the body. It uses practices like acupuncture, herbal medicine, and Qigong to maintain a balance of this (yin/yang) energy. Treatments may include Cupping and Moxibustion. Food is used as medicine. TCM doctors may perform diagnostic testing at various pulse points on the wrist before prescribing herbal formulas tailored to the individual in pill, powder, or loose tea form.

Naturopathy: A system that emphasizes a holistic approach to healthcare, using natural methods like diet and lifestyle changes to support the body's natural healing process.

Homeopathy: A system based on the principle of "like cures like," using highly diluted vibrational substances to stimulate the body's self-healing ability. Popular homeopathic Arnica, available in cream or gel, can rapidly relieve bruising, muscle pain, stiffness, and swelling from injuries to osteoarthritis, and has comparable effectiveness to topical ibuprofen.

PERSONAL CARE PRODUCTS

An estimated 350,000 synthetic chemicals and plastics permeate the planet, with more than 2,000 new chemicals entering the global market each year. "Forever chemicals" like

PFAS (per-and polyfluoroalkyl substances) are found in our water and do not break down easily in the human body or the environment.

Women are exposed to the most toxins from cosmetics, hair and nail care products.

See: Skin Deep, by the Environmental Working Group (EWG), a safe personal care product database site. Help EWG remove cancer-causing chemicals from personal care products. An estimated 350,000 synthetic chemicals and plastics permeate the planet, with more than 2,000 new chemicals entering the global market each year.

Ancients used safe cosmetics like kohl, the black Egyptian eyeliner used by everyone to reduce glare from the sun, to keep the eyes cool & clean. The ancient cosmetic was made from fat, pulverized soot (kohl), and other substances, which provided protection from dust, insects, and various bacterial infections, and also made the eyes more expressive. Eyeshadows were created by pulverized minerals such as malachite, lapis lazuli, or turquoise.

Nail Salon Dangers

Nail salons use chemicals with toxic substances like toluene, formaldehyde, and dibutyl phthalate linked to health issues such as respiratory problems, headaches, and reproductive harm. Chronic frequent exposure in poorly ventilated salons can pose health risks to both workers and customers. Increasingly, salons are choosing to use "3-free" or "5-free" nail polishes, which reduce the use of these harmful chemicals.

An alternative is to just file nails and buff them to a shine using a buffer sponge.

Essential Oils

Whole books are written on the benefits of natural essential oils used topically or inhaled in aromatherapy. A few have safety issues, so do research before using them.

Perfumes from essential oils, alone or in blends, are lovely and have been used in cosmetics, perfumes, and drugs for spiritual, hygienic, and ritualistic purposes since ancient civilizations.

Any "fragrance" is made from synthetic chemicals that can hide hundreds of chemicals, including those linked to endocrine disruption, respiratory issues, and cancer. But individuals may have an allergic reaction to even mild natural essential oils, like lavender, so always skin-test first.

Synthetic Clothing & Microplastics

Microplastics from synthetic fibers like acrylic, polyester and nylon materials are made from petrochemicals and are often formulated with harmful chemical additives like phthalates and bisphenols. New research shows that sweat leaches chemical additives from plastics, and those chemicals are then absorbed through our skin, polluting our water as clothes are laundered. The fibers are in human organs and are damaging to sea life.

END OF LIFE OPTIONS

Donations To Science

Organ donation to science can be designated on your driver's license. In 2025 donation of ligaments is valued at over $5,000 for these high-demand tissues. Donating your body may save a life or contribute significantly to medical research and education, while advancing the development of new treatments and surgical techniques.

Plan Ahead: Make a will and/or set up a living trust that specifies your wishes. You can choose greener options to standard casket burial or cremation. If you make arrangements in advance, you can yet your wishes are documented and save your loved ones stress.

Organ Donor: Designate yourself as an organ donor on your driver's license.

Body Donation: Your body may be able to help someone else. Remains can be cremated and returned to the family.

Cremation Alternatives

Green Burial: Bodies can be buried in a biodegradable shroud or coffin, minimizing environmental impact by avoiding embalming fluids, non-biodegradable caskets, and concrete vaults.

Human Composting: (Natural Organic Reduction) This process transforms the body into nutrient-rich soil. This process is legal in 14 US States: Arizona, California, Colorado, Delaware, Georgia, Maine, Maryland, Minnesota, Nevada, New Jersey, New York, Oregon, Vermont, & Washington. My

Unitarian Universalist Church plans to make this option available to members.

Alkaline Hydrolysis (Aquamation): Known as water cremation, this is a flame-free, eco-friendly alternative to traditional cremation that uses water, heat, and an alkaline solution to break down the body. It produces fewer emissions and uses less energy than flame cremation.

Chapter Eleven
GREEN LIFESTYLES

"If it can't be reduced, reused, repaired, rebuilt, refurbished, refinished, resold, recycled, or composted, then it should be restricted, redesigned, or removed from production."
-PETE SEEGER

As environmental concerns grow more pressing, many individuals are seeking ways to minimize their impact on the planet. A green lifestyle, emphasizes sustainability and mindfulness in daily choices to contribute to individual and environmental sustainability. Each small action, whether it's shifting your diet, changing your commuting habits, or altering your consumption patterns, can collectively create a significant impact.

SYNTHETIC CLOTHING & MICROPLASTICS

Clothing & Microplastics from synthetic fibers like acrylic, polyester and nylon our polluting our water as clothes are laundered. The fibers are in human organs and are damaging to sea life. If you have synthetic clothes, gently hand-wash or wash in laundry bags designed to filter microplastics.

Polyester now makes up over half of all fiber production. Americans dispose of approximately 37 billion tons of used textiles annually, while only 2.5 million garments are donated. Clothing donated to thrift stores in the US exceeds what they can sell. African countries no longer want their shipments.

Synthetic fibers contribute 10% of global carbon emissions, produce 92 million tons of textile waste annually, and consume vast amounts of water, with some estimates showing they are responsible for 20% of global industrial wastewater pollution. 85% of textiles end up in landfills and 500,000 tons of microplastics enter the oceans every year.

In the ocean, microplastics are ingested by a wide range of marine organisms, from plankton to fish and larger marine mammals, and accumulate in humans who consume seafood. Choose fish that is wild-caught, from clean, deep water and choose the muscle tissue in fish fillets, where the guts have been removed. Opting for species like salmon, silver hake, cod, and haddock for lower microplastics. Consciously farmed catfish, barramundi, and trout may also have fewer contaminants. Check on current research.

Natural fibers: Choose natural fibers such as cotton, linen, wool, silk, hemp, and bamboo which offer numerous advantages over synthetic materials. Newer, more sustainable versions of lycra's elastic properties using renewable corn-based ingredients are emerging.

These natural fibers not only enhance comfort and breathability but also promote sustainability, making them preferable choices for clothing that is both stylish and eco-conscious:

Cotton is breathable, soft, and highly absorbent, making it ideal for everyday wear.

Wool stands out for its warmth, elasticity, and ability to regulate temperature. Types of wool include ultra-soft

Cashmere, lustrous Mohair from Angora goats, hypoallergenic Alpaca, fine Merino and rare Vicuna.

Linen, derived from the flax plant, is prized for its durability and moisture-wicking properties, providing comfort in hot climates.

Hemp, known for its durability, strength and resilience, gets softer with each wash and is also environmentally friendly.

Bamboo fiber, popular for its antibacterial properties and moisture management, is sustainable and soft against the skin.

Wild or Raw Silk offers wild silk offer the lowest impact, raw silk is matte and nubby, and processed silk has luxurious softness and a natural sheen. One pound of raw silk requires about 2,500 cocoons, so treat your silk clothing with care.

GREENING ENTERTAINMENT

Considerations to make your entertainment more environment-tally conscious:

Dining out: Find restaurants that offer plates and utensils, or take-out restaurants with biodegradable food containers.

To-go ware: Carry stainless steel nesting lunch boxes for travel and restaurant leftovers.

Recycle: Some takeout containers are reusable and can be easily cleaned.

Water bottles: Use your own reusable water bottles.

Stream programming: On a computer, tablet, smartphone, or small TV.

Indoor entertainment: read books from a library, friends or buy e-books.

Radio: listen to wind-up or solar-powered radios.

Games: organize regular games with neighbors: Poker, Canasta, Bridge, and Hearts. Bingo. There are now permanent Bingo cards which avoid disposable single sheets of paper and markers.

Neighborhood block party: potluck, dance, karaoke,

Zoom or FaceTime events: using these technologies to attend events virtually reduces travel-related carbon emissions. A Zoom call can be set up for a wedding or anniversary to share with long-distance loved ones without travel.

Community Theater & performance: act, sing, dance, or play music in or attend local events.

Event hosting considerations: use sustainable decorations, encourage carpooling, and use local vendors. Prioritize paper plates and bioplastics. Have a DIY washing station for reusables.

GREEN HOBBIES

General Hobbies: Permaculture Gardening, Foraging and Herbalism, Bird watching, Photography & Nature Journaling.

Creative Outlets: Paint, Dance, Sing, Play or learn an instrument. Journaling, writing a memoir or creative writing fosters self-expression.

Brain Activities: Try Puzzles, Games, Meditation, Breath Work, and Mindfulness, take Classes (Online or In-Person).

GREEN CRAFTS

Up-cycling discarded items like cardboard, paper, plastic, glass, and fabric into artworks diverts these materials from recycling or landfills into collages, sculptures, paper-mache masks or puppets, and mixed-media art.

Up-cycled Paper & Fabric Crafts: Use recycled paper and greeting cards or calendar images for Origami, scrapbooking, greeting cards or collage. Vintage clothing can be creatively reused for years. Repurpose old fabrics and clothing to create new items, such as quilts, bags, or throw pillows. Up-cycle recycled cigar boxes into keepsake storage, painted and decorated with paper. Turn single socks into hand puppets, transform glass jars into decorative storage.

PAPER CRAFTS

Greeting Cards: DIY cards for all occasions.

Cutting Paper Shapes: like snowflakes.

Scrapbooking: preserve memories in an album.

Origami: paper folding to make a paper crane, owl, star or flower.

Paper Bead Jewelry: Paper beads made from rolled-up, long triangles of color images from magazines with wheat paste glue to create oval beads.

FIBER CRAFTS

Sewing, Knitting, Crochet, Embroidery, Lace making, & Quilting

Felting: Felting techniques matt wool fibers together to make a solid fabric.

Weaving: Weaving is an ancient craft of interlacing natural materials for baskets and shelters, with its development into cloth-making. Cotton is the most commonly natural fiber, and wool is the most common animal fiber sourced from sheep, goats, alpaca and other animals.

Natural Dyes: Natural dyes come from plants, fruits, and vegetables to dye fabrics, paper, and other materials. Solar dyeing is the most ecologically friendly and kind to natural fibers, such as silk and wool, used in fiber arts. To solar dye, you need sun and warm weather to heat the fibers in a dye bath in glass jars for hours to days.

NATURE CRAFTS

Handcrafts: Carving Wood or Stone, Woodworking & Jewelry making.

Dried botanicals: Some plants can be dried for use and dried arrangements. Wreath-making can use a fiber or wire frame to hold evergreens or an edible wreath of bay leaf, oregano &

rosemary. Garlic braids, strings of chiles, or other classic kitchen decorative edibles.

Beeswax Candles: Avoid petroleum-based paraffin candles. Beeswax candles are the superior choice. They are pleasant-smelling, non-toxic, burn longer, brighter & cleaner.

They emit negative ions that help neutralize pollutants and purify the air. Beeswax is a biodegradable, renewable resource. Bees are vital for pollination, so using beeswax supports beekeepers and their bee work, helping maintain ecosystems.

Clays: Natural clay is Earth-friendly, but firing clay is energy-intensive and best reserved for utility ceramic products.

Air-dry Clay: is made from natural clay minerals, water, and binders like paper and glue, which air-dry at room temperature but will dissolve in water unless sealed. Avoid Polymer clay, which is made of plastic.

Up-cycled Furniture: Refinish or refurbish old furniture to create new home décor pieces. Repaint old chairs with antiquing treatments or stenciled designs using latex paint.

Leatherwork once processed it is less hazardous. There are non-toxic dyes available.

Glass blowing: This requires access to a class at a glass-blowing studio with a high-temperature furnace, glory hole, and annealer, plus a complete set of tools. The process is energy-intensive and best reserved for products of beauty and utility that have a long life, like drinkware, vases, and collectible home decor.

PAINTS

Acrylic paint dangers: Water-soluble acrylic paints have become popular for their bright colors. The manufacturing of acrylics is an energy-intensive, petroleum-based process that causes GHG emissions that can pollute groundwater and drinking water supplies. Acrylic paints contain air-polluting Volatile Organic Compounds (VOCs) and phthalates, both harmful to the user artist and the environment.

Acrylic paint additives, alkyl phenol ethoxylates (APEs), are suspected carcinogens and endocrine disruptors that can harm humans, animals, and sea life. Acrylic paints also contribute to microplastic pollution when washed down the drain. All rinse water should be collected in a bucket to dehydrate into a solid piece of plastic that may take centuries to break down, slowing its negative effects.

Most paints intended for children are certified non-toxic. Professional-grade art materials may contain toxic pigments, such as cadmium and cobalt, which can be harmful if ingested or inhaled (as dust) or cause skin irritation.

Water-based paints: watercolors, water-soluble pencils, gouache, casein, and tempera are all inherently low-VOC or zero-VOC. You can substitute white latex house paint for gesso to prime a canvas. Avoid modern acrylic gesso. Latex is durable and low-odor.

Oil Paints & Oil Pastel sticks: Thinning classic oil paints requires linseed oil or walnut oil, and/or solvents like Grumbacher's Grumtine, a renewable, bio-based substitute for turpentine for both thinning paint and cleaning equipment. But brushes can be cleaned with soap and water. The soapy water can be dehydrated in a container for disposal.

Notc that "natural" does not necessarily mean "harmless," and solvents require proper handling and disposal. Turpentine, the traditional and powerful solvent originally derived from pine resin, is now commonly a petroleum-derived product. Odorless mineral spirits (OMS) are not odorless.

Water-Soluble Oil Paint: Grumbacher's MAX oils are made water-soluble by adding a modified linseed oil that acts as an emulsifier. Add a final art varnish that is non-toxic, low-VOC, water-based & plant-based: like Grumvar Gloss varnish or Natural Earth Paint.

WATER MEDIA

Most water media can last a long time because dried paint can be rehydrated, unlike dried acrylic and oil paints. The drawback is that water can damage the finished art, which requires framing under glass with a protective paper mat.

Transparent Watercolor: Known for its transparency and luminosity, it is pigment suspended in a water-soluble binder, such as gum arabic.

Gouache: a.k.a. opaque watercolor or designer colors, also uses gum arabic binder with chalk added to make it opaque with a matte finish.

Casein: A milk protein-based paint that uses milk curd as the binder which becomes insoluble after curing.

Poster Paint (Tempera) was originally made with egg yolk, but is now made with pigments, starch and cellulose. Some pigments, such as cadmium, cobalt, and lead, are toxic if ingested.

Gesso: Gesso was made from chalk or gypsum and a binder. Avoid modern Acrylic gesso, which uses an acrylic emulsion as the binder, and substitute white latex house paint to prime a canvas.

Latex Paint: Primarily used for interior and exterior house painting, it is a water-based medium that is durable and low-odor. Around 75% of all paint sales are latex-based due to the easier cleanup with soap and water, faster drying times, and improved durability with better color retention. Caution: While many house paints are still called "latex," they are often made with a higher percentage of acrylic polymers.

House Paints: Environmental regulations on volatile organic compounds (VOCs) have also contributed to the decline of oil-based paints. Being water-based, they contain fewer VOCs than oil-based paints, making them a less toxic and more environmentally friendly option.

Reduce waste: Only buy the amount of paint you need and look for brands that use recycled content or offer sustainable options.

DRAWING MEDIA

Pencils: Pencil cores do not contain lead and are non-toxic. They use a mixture of finely ground graphite and clay. Softer pencils have more graphite, resulting in a darker line, while harder pencils contain more clay and produce a lighter line.

Water-soluble Pencils: These are colored pencils, graphite, or pastels formulated with water-soluble binders.

Oil-based Colored Pencils: Artist-grade colored pencil cores are made from pigment, oil, and other binders, making them hard and resistant to breaking.

Pencil types: These include charcoal, graphite pencils graded for hardness/softness (H-B scale) for different uses, and oil-based or water-soluble colored pencils. Crayons use wax or oil as a binder and include wax, oil, and paper-wrapped crayons.

Charcoal: Charcoal art sticks are highly compressed, intensely black crayons made from burnt willow or vine. Fixatives are required to prevent it from smudging the finished art. Use casein (milk protein) and grain alcohol-based odorless Spectra-fix spray, safe to use indoors, or DIY fixative: a weak solution of milk and vodka.

Wax–Based Crayons: Wax crayons are typically non-toxic.

Pastel chalks: soft, hard & oil pastels: These are artist-quality, highly pigmented sticks created with a binder for a wide range of colors and applications.

Conté Crayons: Conté crayons are compressed rectangular sticks made from graphite or charcoal, with colored pigments and a clay or wax binder, invented by the Frenchman Nicholas-Jacque Conté.

Natural chalks: Natural chalks are mined minerals. Common white chalk is calcium carbonate, mined from fine-grained limestone.

Colored Sidewalk chalk is more temporary, and modern options include chalk markers and sprays.

INKS

Algae ink uses pigment from algae waste cells, making it carbon-negative. It sequesters carbon, reduces water use, and avoids petroleum-based pigments, unlike most other inks that still rely on fossil fuels for their colorants. It is available in both water and soy-based carriers. Water-based inks are Low VOC.

Art & Creative Materials Institute (ACMI) certified colored drawing inks are nontoxic and safe for normal use. Certain Tattoo inks may contain heavy metals or industrial-grade pigments, such as those found in printer toner or car paint, which can be harmful.

India ink: A water-based ink, and many modern specialized India inks are formulated with bio-based ingredients, using regenerative, sustainable pigments.

Colored inks: Used for illustrations and calligraphy, these inks are non-toxic.

Tattoo inks: Can be toxic because they often contain chemicals like heavy metals, carcinogens, and allergens, as well as potential microbial contaminants.

Graphite: Natural graphite, formed from the metamorphism of carbonaceous rocks, or manufactured synthetic graphite, provides the base material. This graphite is then mixed with a binder that allows it to dissolve in water, creating a medium that can be used dry, like a pencil, or activated with water to blend like watercolor paint.

NEW GREEN Rs

Reduce: ask if you really need it

Rethink: how we can create enjoyable, greener lifestyles

Reuse: buy for durability and prioritize biologically based products

Reject: fossil fuel-based products

Recycle: recycle all your biodegradable materials, metals, and glass.

Repair: fix it until it can't be repaired, and then recycle the materials

Renew or Refurbish: clean, repaint, reupholster, touch-up cosmetic blemishes

www.ingramcontent.com/pod-product-compliance
Lightning Source LLC
LaVergne TN
LVHW022051200926
848481LV00003B/863

* 9 7 9 8 2 9 5 5 3 3 7 9 2 *